CARE OF THE
STABLED HORSE

CARE OF THE STABLED HORSE

David Hamer

B.T. Batsford Ltd · London

First published 1993

© David Hamer, 1993

Typeset by Goodfellow & Egan Ltd, Cambridge
and printed in Great Britain by Butler and Tanner,
Frome, Somerset

Published by
B.T. Batsford Ltd
4 Fitzhardinge Street
London W1H 0AH

A CIP catalogue record for this book is available
from the British Library

ISBN 0 7134 6998 6

CONTENTS

ACKNOWLEDGEMENTS

My thanks are due to all those who have guided me and taught me good stable management; in particular Doris Culshaw and Josephine Batty-Smith; for this book results from their knowledge.

My thanks are also due to Sophie Edwards and Jayne Gould for helping me to compile the final text, and to my long-suffering colleagues; Sheila Roughton, Clare Hill and Derek Payne, who have endured my fits of frustration whilst typing the manuscript, and to Mr P.S. Hastie MRCVS for advice on parts of the text.

All photographs are by Richard Hamer unless otherwise stated.

Technical line diagrams are by Carole Vincer and the part-title illustrations are by Gabrielle Ceriden Morse.

FOREWORD

The most successful stable management is achieved by a complete understanding of the physical and mental needs of the horse; both in his wild state and under stabled conditions.

The horse has served mankind for generations in many different ways. In modern times he is caught up in a high powered world of money and sport, as well as giving thousands of people a great deal of pleasure, some of whom have not come from a background in horse management from which they could learn.

Highly sophisticated training techniques of the present day have to be matched by an increased knowledge of the feeding, travelling, shoeing and general day-to-day care of the competition horse, race horse and hunter. Even horses and ponies that are not put under the pressure of competitive work suffer stresses and strains from the environment in which we expect them to live.

If there are any flaws within this most necessary care and attention, the valued success by which our life with horses is monitored will not be achieved or maintained.

Having read *Care of the Stabled Horse*, I am sure that experienced horse people, students seeking knowledge for exams and all those who are starting out as first time horse owners, will benefit from the wealth of information and detail to be found in this book.

Now more than ever in this world of machinery, pollution, over crowding, and technology, the horse deserves to be looked after in the best possible way. Any person absorbing the knowledge in the following pages will be able to do so.

Tricia Gardiner FBHS
Little Somerford, Wilts, 1992

PREFACE

The correct care of horses is a subject that has prompted many authors over the years to put pen to paper. Good management of the horse; be it in the stable or in the field, is vital to its well-being. The modern horse has many demands made of it and with the increasing growth of competitive events, it is expected to perform at times to both its physical and mental limits. However, the basic skills and meticulous attention to detail required for good management apply for *all* horses; performance or not. In this book I have endeavoured to study the horse with a broad view. The horse owner needs to have an understanding of the horse both physically and mentally, as well as of the effects of domestication. Where relevant, I have included notes on the horse's physiology to give some understanding to the good practices required. However, theory will not replace practical experience and so the reader should apply this knowledge to their work, and not become a self-appointed veterinary surgeon or psycho-analyst. The person that cares for the stabled or grass-kept horse must be prepared to accept the discipline and responsibility involved. Their reward: a healthy, content and willing partner – the horse.

Part 1
CREATING A HEALTHY ENVIRONMENT

1

HORSE PSYCHOLOGY

The domestication of horses dates back to the third millennium BC. Prior to this period, man had hunted the horse as a source of food.

Through the centuries, man has developed a special relationship with the horse, first as a partner in work and war and later for recreation.

Despite centuries of domestication, the horse's natural instincts are as strong as that of his ancestor, the Eohippus that roamed and grazed the plains of a prehistoric world. The strongest natural instinct of the horse is his quick and sometimes violent reaction to change. This instinct can have a considerable effect on the horse's well-being; particularly when we first stable him, or move him from one yard to another.

The physiology of the horse has evolved over thousands of years to cope with the requirements that have been and are still being made of him. However, today's horse still has much in common with his ancestors, such as his swiftness to move across land or away from danger; and his small stomach and long intestinal tract to cope with continual browsing of grass and fibre, and to allow him to move at speed.

Man has a tendency to 'humanize' domesticated animals and in doing so, expects animals to display the reasoning, logic and reactions of another person. In this way, little account is made for the horse's mental state or feelings, as man expects the horse to rationalize and 'work things out' as he would himself. This is often seen in the way in which some people handle their horses, blaming a horse's lack of co-operation or poor performance on its personality.

Horses are gregarious animals, and have a strong herding instinct (1). They work well together and sometimes can be difficult to handle if separated from a longtime companion. It is not natural for horses to live alone, and they may well become dull and dejected. Human company is poor compensation.

The Senses

The natural senses of the horse are well developed, particularly his smell, taste, hearing and touch. However, the horse's sight is not as well developed as in other animals. The setting of the eyes on the side of the head allows for a wide field of vision to spot oncoming predators. A mobile neck also helps to compensate for the horse's poor ability to focus, and enables him to see from a distance. The

1a, 1b Despite their domestication by man, horses are happiest in each others' company

horse's sight does not react quickly from light to dark, so he is naturally nervous of dark or shady areas. The sixth sense is an unknown quantity. The horse does have an uncanny ability to react to a person's temperament and personality. A horse will soon become wary of someone who is aggressive, but can be calmed by someone who is quiet and confident. Horses also 'sense' imminent events by picking up 'vibrations' from their human companions. Why do some horses always seem to know when they are going to competitions before you have even started to prepare them? When a horse's mental state is unstable, his senses will be exaggerated. By stabling the horse, we hinder his instinct for flight, and some horses will worry themselves to such an extent that their condition and general well-being suffers.

Handling horses

It is certainly true that some people have 'a way with horses'. This could be that the horse's sixth sense perceives a kind, calm and gentle personality. Horses require consistency (2), they react badly to stressful or changeable circumstances and erratic handling. The handler must be quiet and confident. Nervousness or aggression will be detected quickly by the horse. Safety is of paramount importance when handling horses. Liberties should not be taken, even with the older, more 'sensible' horse. Tying the horse up when working with him in the stable creates a controlled situation in which both handler and horse can gain confidence.

There are few 'evil' horses. Ill-temper is usually the result of poor handling. Horses are individuals: they can be ner-

Fig. 1 Keen, alert, and ready for flight

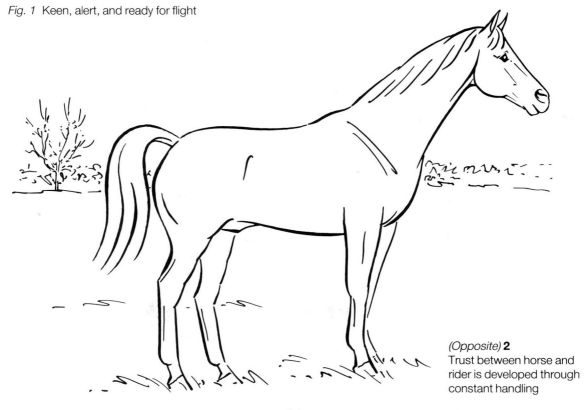

(Opposite) **2**
Trust between horse and rider is developed through constant handling

vous, stubborn, cowardly or brave. Some may seem stupid, whilst others are intelligent. If a horse is difficult, his handler must consider the reason; this could be ill-treatment, over-indulgence, physical discomfort, or simply an excess of youthful high spirits.

We must learn to judge how a horse is feeling by his stance and facial expression (**fig. 1**)

Punishment and reward

Occasionally a horse will behave badly for no apparent reason; in such cases punishment is justified. However, horses have good memories, so rough and violent treatment will be long remembered. They should never be smacked on the head, not even as a slap on the nose in retaliation to a nip, as the horse may become head-shy. The timing of the punishment is important, as the horse must relate it to the misbehaviour; it is pointless to limp away from a horse that has kicked you and to return later to punish it, as the horse will by then have forgotten his misdemeanour. It is important to get your timing right, whether administering punishment, or reward. Horses respond better to encouragement, so whenever possible try to achieve your end by reward.

Behavioural Problems

Stable vices

In his wild state, the horse rarely develops the 'vices' seen in many stabled horses. Habits such as weaving, cribbiting, wind-sucking and box-walking are particularly associated with highly-strung and sensitive horses, particularly when there has been some change or disturbance around them.

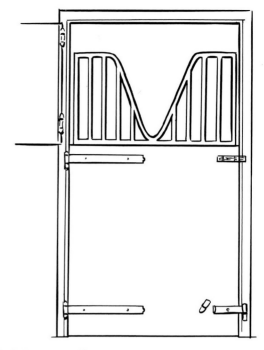

Fig. 2 Anti-weave grill

Weaving The horse swings his head and neck from side to side, rocking from one foreleg to another. This is usually done over the stable door. Anti-weave grills can help, but some horses will weave behind them (**fig. 2**).

Crib-biting and Wind-sucking These vices are usually found together (although some horses just chew wood). The horse grabs a fixed object with his front teeth, (often the door top or a fixed manger), arches his neck and sucks in air. Horses that crib bite often have very worn front teeth. A horse windsucks by shaking his head violently up and down, and sucking in air. Cribbing can be controlled by putting a 'crib strap' on the horse (**fig. 3**), or by an operation in which the surgeon removes a section of the muscles at the top underside of the neck, and cuts the nerve supply to that area. This operation has a variable success rate.

Box-walking The horse will be very restless, and continually walking round and round his box. He will often work himself into a sweat, and will generally lose condition. Sometimes, just moving the horse to another stable can help.

Boredom can also have a poor effect on the horse's state of mind, and horses can develop peculiar habits to while away the hours. When considering this problem, one should remember the horse's browsing instinct that drives him to wander in search of food. It is better for a horse to have regular small intakes of high-fibre food to keep his mental state good and his digestive system healthy.

Temperament difficulties

These are usually man-made, by bad handling or just by putting the horse in an unnatural environment, such as a stable. Some breeds can be more highly strung than others, although it is often 'cross-bred' horses that are the most difficult.

Certainly, mares can be troublesome, particularly when in season. This can be countered by using drugs to control their oestrus cycle. However, few people grant mares the same respect when handling them that they would a stallion. Remember that mares are entires too, so their handling requires more patience than that of a gelding.

Horses must be allowed to adapt gradually to change, with their natural life-style and instinct being taken into account. They must be handled in a consistently calm and confident way. We should allow for the individuality and personality of each horse and above all we must respect them as we would any partner or friend.

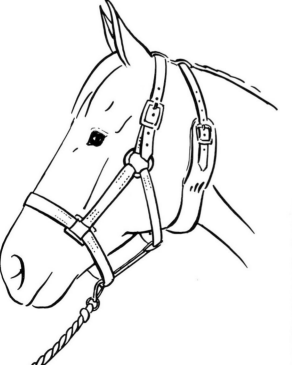

Fig. 3 Crib strap fitted

SUMMARY

- Horses' natural instincts affect their behaviour when they are stabled.
- They must be handled in a quiet and confident way.
- They react better to encouragement than punishment.
- Stable vices are often due to boredom or mental distress.

2
BRINGING THE HORSE UP FROM GRASS

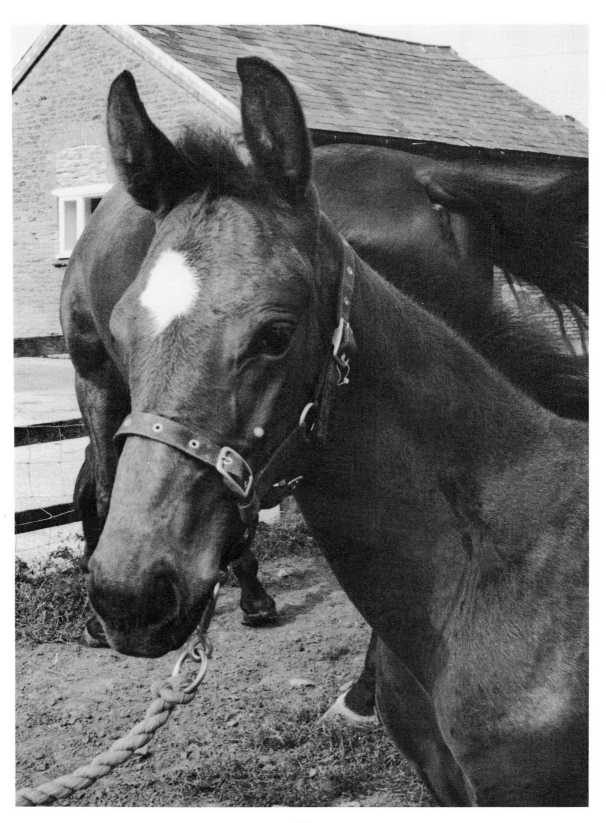

2
BRINGING THE HORSE UP FROM GRASS

For a variety of reasons, people turn their horses away for rest and relaxation at grass. Some people argue that it is unhealthy for a horse to be worked to peak fitness and then allowed to become fat and unfit in a field, only to be brought back into work and fitness at a later stage. Keeping a horse fit definitely lengthens his life. Like people, it is healthier for a horse to be kept lean and active.

However, we must think again about the horse's psychological state, and appreciate the benefits of a period of rest for those horses that have been under mental and physical stress, such as eventers, hunters and other competition horses. It is up to us to get the balance right between giving a well-earned break and allowing a horse to run to fat. Turning your horses away for a short period can also give you the chance to organize and sort out your yard. It is certainly not necessary to give a horse a long break in the field if he is in light work and goes out on a daily basis.

The time of year that you bring your horse up from grass will vary depending on the type of work that you and your horse do.

Hunters These are brought up at the beginning of August to allow enough time for a fitness programme that will prepare them for the opening meet, which is traditionally the first Saturday in November.

Eventers The timing varies, depending in which season they compete; it can be spring, summer, or autumn. Usually, they are turned away during the winter and brought up from grass in the New Year.

Dressage horses and show jumpers These horses are usually given a break as and when they need one. Their season runs all year, and good management is required to keep them fresh. Often this type of horse is not turned away as such, just his work varied.

Show horses Usually these horses will begin preparation for the show ring in the early spring. They may have spent the winter doing other activities such as hunting, or competition work.

Polo ponies Their season starts in May, so they will be brought up in the New Year.

Preparing to Bring Up Your Horse from Grass

The stable yard

This should have already been given its annual 'spring clean' while the horses are out, which is also a good opportunity to do any necessary repairs. Horses are notorious vandals, and each year you will have quite a bit of patching up and painting to do. At the end of the last season, the stable should have been cleared out and disinfected. All fire appliances should have been checked and serviced.

Fodder, feed and bedding

Hay This is often best stored in an open-sided barn and the best value is to be had by buying the hay off the field in the summer. A horse eats roughly three to four bales of hay a week, and you are wise to order enough to last the entire season, particularly if your horse is to be stabled through January to March, as later in the season hay can become scarce and expensive. There are alternatives to hay on the market, which have different feed values for specific purposes. Whatever you like to feed, it is better to feed good quality meadow hay for the first three to four weeks, as this will make the change of diet from grass to hard feed more gradual. You should mix in the hay that you will feed permanently with the meadow hay after the first two weeks.

Hard feed This has a finite 'shelf life' and should be bought accordingly. Many modern feeds are compounds sweetened with syrup to encourage the horse to eat them. This can make it difficult to tell when the feed is off. As a rule of thumb, feed should generally be used within a month, or sooner in hot climates.

Bedding This is covered later in Chapter 4. Basically, you should have ordered enough of the correct bedding in advance to last the season. The more dust-free the bedding, the better for the horse's health.

Saddlery and equipment

Saddle This should have been to the saddler to have the stitching checked and to be re-flocked if necessary. Flock is the term used to describe the stuffing used in the saddle, and stems from the time when saddles were stuffed with sheep wool. It is important to have your saddle re-flocked at least once a year, to ensure that the rider's weight is distributed evenly on the horse's back. If it is not, many problems can occur, such as bad backs for both horse and rider, and possible damage to the tree of the saddle.

Bridle This, along with the other equipment, should have had any damaged stitching repaired.

Rugs There are many different types of rug available on the market today. Whichever type of rugs you use, they must be clean and in good repair before the season starts. You should clean and wash all rugs as soon as you have finished with them, as the horse's urine will rot many types of fibre.

Clipping machine and blades These should have been sent back to the manufacturer at the end of the last season, to service the machine and sharpen the blades. It can take some time, so it is too late to think about it just when you need to use them!

General health

Vaccinations It is a good idea to have these done before the horse is brought

into serious work. Some horses do not react well to influenza vaccination, and it is not always convenient to let the horse have a period of rest during the season. Influenza vaccinations should be given every six to eight months to horses that travel to a large number of shows, as this will provide better immunity.

Teeth It is essential to have the horse's teeth checked and rasped at least once a year. Older horses may need doing more often. Many problems are caused by sharp molar teeth such as failing to keep condition on your horse, or being unable to get the horse to accept a contact when ridden. It is important that the back molars are rasped as well, so your vet will need the necessary equipment (**17**) (see Chapter 5).

Feet The horse's feet should receive regular attention whilst at grass. Some people like to remove the shoes when they turn away their horse, to allow the feet to expand. This is only wise if recommended by your farrier, as some horse's feet (flat feet, for example), are the wrong shape to expand (**3**). Furthermore, if the ground is hard, feet can break up and cause lameness. It is generally better to remove the hind shoes and keep front shoes on (**4**). This protects the forefeet, which carry the most weight, and will stop the horse from damaging others if he kicks.

Feed The horse's digestive system is very sensitive, and any dietary changes must be gradual. Try to introduce small amounts of the concentrate feed that you will use in the stable whilst the horse is still at grass, so that the microbes in the horse's hind gut can adjust to the change in diet. By mid-August the nutritional value of grass is fairly low anyway, so some horses may require additional feeds to keep them in condition.

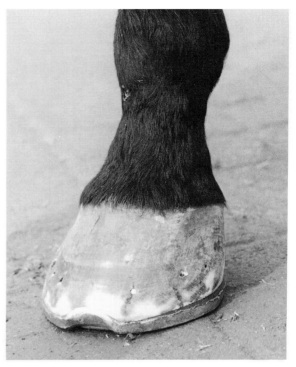

3 Horses with flat feet need shoes

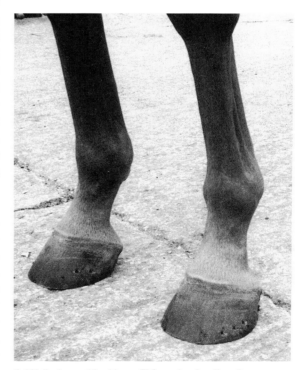

4 Well-shaped feet benefit from having the shoes removed once in a while

The First Three Weeks

Week one

Management Bring the horse in to the stable during the day. He may be shod all round if necessary. Wash his saddle and girth area with salt water (50g (2oz) of salt to 0.5l (1pt) of water) to help condition the skin. It is a good idea to put brushing boots and knee pads on the horse when exercising him. He should be on dust-free bedding, such as paper.

Feed Give a small concentrate feed once a day and soaked meadow hay to prevent coughing. Normally, you soak hay for a minimum of eight hours or a maximum of 12. This washes off dust and makes the fungal spores swell up so that they cannot pass down the bronchial tubes into the lungs. Longer periods of soaking will wash the spores off altogether, but also washes away important nutrients. You must watch that the hay does not start to ferment in the water.

Exercise Towards the end of the week, you may walk the horse, walking, for 30–40 minutes. Use a soft numnah (saddle pad) under the saddle and a soft girth, or a girth sleeve over a leather girth. Be careful not to work the horse into a sweat as he may catch a chill easily at this stage. Some people will start their exercise programme with the horse on the lunge. This should be done only if the horse needs to have the edge taken off him before you ride, as working on a circle is quite strenuous to an unfit horse.

Check daily Check that your horse is not rubbing from the tack. He may cough a little at first, but ensuring that his hay is well soaked should relieve this.

Week two

Management Bring the horse in at night and turn out for half of the day. Start to groom the horse more thoroughly to clean his coat and skin, and if it is cold at night put a lightweight run on. Continue washing his girth and saddle area with salt water.

Feed Increase the feed so that you can give three small feeds a day. He should have as much soaked meadow hay as he will eat.

Exercise Continuing the walking exercise, but increase to one hour by the end of the week.

Check daily As week one.

Week three

Management The horse may now be stabled all the time or you may wish to turn him out for a couple of hours daily if you have enough grazing, and this is, without doubt, of great benefit to the horse psychologically. With competition horses, you may find that they 'play' too much in the field as they get fit.

Feed Start to cut the hay ration and increase concentrates. If the horse has become overweight whilst turned away you will need to restrict his feed to help him lose weight.

Exercise Increase to one-and-a-half hours per day. You should now expect the horse to walk quite actively and include some gradients. Hill-work is definitely the best way of strengthening muscles and developing the efficiency of the cardio-vascular system, and can be particularly effective at the slower gaits, so reducing

undue stress on the limbs. You can now include some trotting work, but only two- or three-minute bursts on level going.

Check daily It is important that you check the horse over daily, especially after exercise for any heat in the legs, or for injury. Any warning signs in the early stages can prevent long-term injury. Heat is a sign of increased blood flow, and can indicate inflammation.

SUMMARY

- The change from the field to the stable must be gradual.
- Enough time must be allowed to get the horse fit for his work.
- Careful preparation beforehand can reduce costs and save time.
- In the first three weeks in particular, great attention must be paid to the horse's condition.

3
STABLE
CONSTRUCTION

3

STABLE CONSTRUCTION

Essentially, there are two types of yard: the open yard, in which each stable opens onto the outside; and the barn system, in which the boxes are housed within a building. Whichever system of stabling you choose, you must remember that horses require good ventilation, and you need enough space to move around them easily. Horses have a tendency to get themselves caught up or stuck, if they can, so care should be taken when planning and choosing fixtures.

The Open Yard

This system is popular in Great Britain where the climate is temperate. It can be extremely attractive if well designed (6). It is healthy for the horse, as it allows plenty of ventilation which is so vital to the horse's health. The horse is able to see his surroundings, and disease spreads less easily. The main disadvantage with this system is the amount of extra labour required to keep it. Often there are large areas to sweep and long distances between feed and tackrooms. In bad weather, it is less pleasant to work in.

The Barn System

This system is more common in the USA and in northern Europe, where the winters are very cold. If the building is well planned, it can be an excellent system (5); it is certain to be more labour-saving. Ideally, the horse should still able to look outside, so you may have a half door that can be opened at the back of the box in fine weather or during the summer. The boxes should have full partitions between them as horses tend to squabble, particularly at feed times. Because of the danger of horses getting trapped in the yard in the case of fire, there should be two or more exits. Above all, it is important that the building is spacious enough for the horse's health and for safe working.

Choosing a site

Getting the construction of stables correct is important. When designing them, we must consider safety along with the horse's physical requirements. Also, the stables must be sited in a suitable environment. To ensure this, we must consider the site's location and amenities.

5 A well-planned barn system works well

The locality The first consideration must be 'why are you building the stables?' If it is for commercial reasons, such as a riding school, then you need to do some market research to see if there is a need for such a business in the area. Whatever you build, you will require planning permission and if you do wish to run a riding school, you will need a licence from your local authority.

All animals require supervision. When choosing a site you must consider accommodation for someone to be available to supervise the horses, and offer some security.

Other considerations must be the amount of pure air available. Building in very wooded areas would restrict this, as the trees absorb a great deal of the fresh air. A building near major roads or industrial sites is not good for horses. Finally, it has been found that a horse's performance can be affected by a high pollen count.

When you have decided on a site, make sure that the stable faces away from the prevailing wind, which in the northern hemisphere is south or south-west. This position will also mean that the stables catch as much light as possible.

6 The open yard is an attractive system, if well-designed

Foundations Light sandy soil or gravel give the best foundation. If you live in an area which has clay soil, then you will have to excavate and lay down good, free-draining foundations.

Water and electricity These should be available nearby. If you have to run mains electricity or water to the site, it will be very expensive.

Access With the tremendous increase in horse-related road accidents, it is important that you consider the access to the yard when riding out. Crossing or riding along busy roads is inadvisable, due to the horse's unpredictability in traffic.

The stable

Size This depends on the size of the horse. The average 16hh horse should have a minimum of 3.7 × 3.7m (12 × 12ft). For sick nursing, it is a good idea to have at least 4.3 × 4.3m (14 × 14ft).

Ventilation Horses must have a constant supply of fresh air; remember that the horse's natural habitat is the wide open plain. His large lunge capacity enables him to move at speed, and utilise enough oxygen to enable him to take flight. Horses suffer badly from dust. Signs of lung damage are not often apparent. Even a slight cough when first exercized can mean that there is damage to the lungs. The horse requires at least 43cum (1,500 cu ft) of air space, and the height of the building should be at least 4.5m (15ft) to the apex. Other than the window and door, a form of ventilation system should be installed to circulate the air. Three common types are louvre boards, cowls and ventilator hoods. (**figs. 4, 5, 6**).

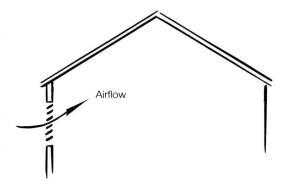

Fig. 4 Louvre boards

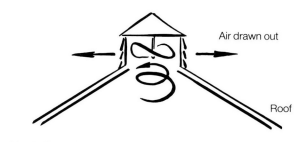

Fig. 5 A cowl system

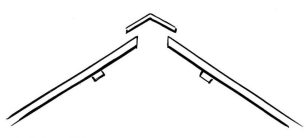

Fig. 6 A ventilator hood

With the barn system, in a hot climate it may be necessary to supplement the ventilation by using electric extractor fans or expensive air-conditioning systems that cool the air.

Floors The most commonly used flooring today is concrete. It is cheap and hard-wearing. If used, it should be grooved to prevent the horse slipping. Traditional stables were built with 'blue brick' flooring. This is vitreous brick that

is waterproof, easy to clean and wears well. It is still available today, but is extremely expensive. Some yards just roll down the clay earth until it is hard. This is not satisfactory as the clay will gradually absorb the urine and become pitted and unlevel. It is possible to lay down rubber matting floors, usually lining the walls as well. This offers extra protection to the horse and may mean that you can put in less bedding. Whichever flooring you use, it is better to have a slight gradient (usually 2.5cm (1 in) in 3.7m (12 ft)), preferably to the back of the box, to enable the horse's urine to drain away through a drainage channel **(fig. 7a)**.

Drains You will need several drains around the yard to take away rainfall, effluent and water used during the day. It is a good idea to design the boxes so that they drain to the back and then into a covered drainage channel (see above). Horses stand at the door for most of the day, so it is not a good idea to drain to the front of the box, as they will stand in soggy bedding, which is not healthy for their feet. All drains should be designed so that they are easy to clean, and that the covers can withstand the weight of a horse.

Walls The walls should be at least 3m (10ft) high, with the first 1.2m (4ft) solid, as horses tend to kick out. The best material, but most expensive, is brick. It is weatherproof, hard-wearing, easily disinfected and provides good insulation, being warm in winter and cool in summer. Cement blocks are a good alternative, although they must be finished properly as they can be very rough. Many stables are built of wood, as it is much cheaper. These should be built on a brick course to prevent rot, and the walls should be lined with solid planking for the

first 1.2m (4ft) **(fig. 7b)**. The problems with wooden stables are that they are a fire risk, horses tend to chew them, and wood is a poor conductor of heat; unless well insulated, they tend to be hot in the summer and cold in the winter. Wood can also harbour disease. Whichever material you use, it is a good idea to run a groove or ridge around the inside of the box at a height of about 1m (3ft 6in) to enable a horse that gets cast against the wall to free itself.

Roofs Slates or roofing tiles are the best material as they reduce the fire risk and keep an even temperature all year around. Corrugated iron is sometimes used, but is not very satisfactory as it is noisy and gets extremely hot in summer. Roofing felt is quite common, especially with wooden boxes. It does need to be renewed regularly (every eight to ten years) and increases the fire risk. In the open yard system, it is a good idea to have a 0.6m (2ft) overhang over the stable door to keep the horse's head dry and to make it easier to work around the stables in wet weather **(fig. 7b)**.

Windows These are usually on the same side as the doors, to prevent a through draught. You may wish to have a small window at the back of the box as well, to open in the summer and increase ventilation.

The windows should be high enough that the horse cannot get his legs through them. Most windows have glass panes and these should be covered with metal grills that the horse cannot get through or become caught up in.

Windows should be able to be opened: they are there to provide ventilation as well as light. It is possible to buy toughened clear plastic instead of glass which means that you do not need to cover them.

a Plan

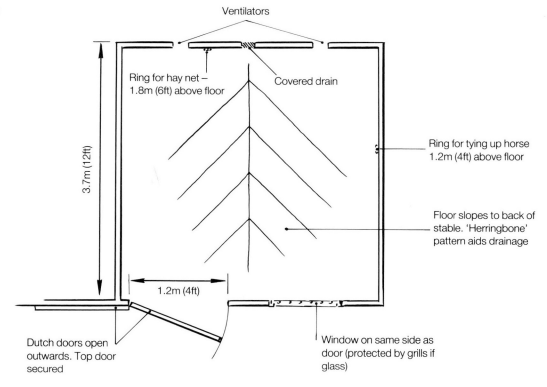

Ventilators

Ring for hay net –
1.8m (6ft) above floor

Covered drain

3.7m (12ft)

Ring for tying up horse
1.2m (4ft) above floor

Floor slopes to back of
stable. 'Herringbone'
pattern aids drainage

1.2m (4ft)

Dutch doors open
outwards. Top door
secured

Window on same side as
door (protected by grills if
glass)

b Side elevation

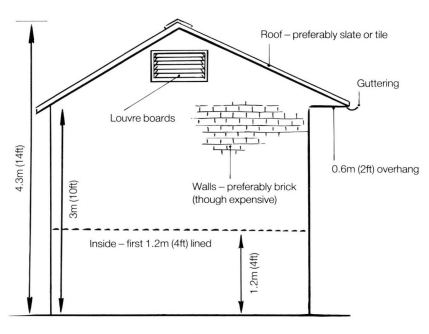

Roof – preferably slate or tile

Guttering

4.3m (14ft)

3m (10ft)

Louvre boards

Walls – preferably brick
(though expensive)

0.6m (2ft) overhang

Inside – first 1.2m (4ft) lined

1.2m (4ft)

Fig. 7a Stable construction – Plan

Fig. 7b Stable construction – Side Elevation

Fig. 8 Barn system

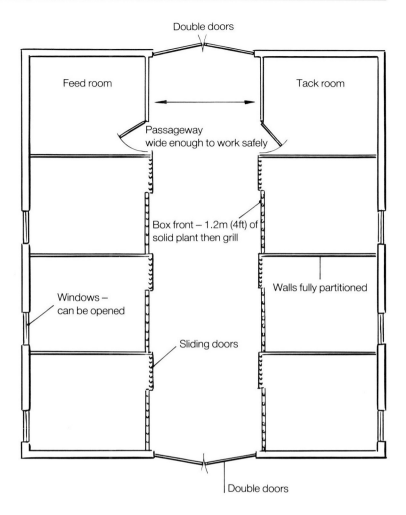

Doors With the open yard system, it is best to have Dutch doors. These have each door in two halves, usually with the bottom door slightly larger than the top. The doorway should be at least 2.4m (8ft) high and about 1.2m (4ft) wide to accommodate the average horse. Low, narrow doorways encourage a horse to rush through, and often cause them to panic and pull back as you approach them. The horse can also seriously damage himself if he catches his flank or hip on the door. The top and inside of the bottom door should be lined to stop the horse chewing it. Zinc is the best metal to use, but it is very expensive. Most people use a form of galvanized tin.

In barn systems, there are various types of door used, but the best is hung on the top frame so that it can slide open. The doors can be fully grilled or have anti-weave bars to enable the horse to look out. It is possible to have Dutch doors, but this is not always ideal, as they can block passageways.

Whichever type of door you use, it must be hinged or hung so that it opens outwards in case a horse gets trapped in the box and you need to get in (**fig. 8**).

Bolts and fastenings These must be 'horse-proof'. Some horses are very clever at escaping from their stables. There are various designs on the market. Two bolts

are usually best, one at the top and one at the bottom (it is best if the latter can be operated by your foot).

Fixtures and fittings This area can be a subject of great debate. Some people feel that these should be kept to a minimum, as horses may injure themselves or get caught up in them. Undoubtedly, all fixtures and fittings must be safe, and placed so that they cause no harm to the horse.

Rings A tie-up ring is essential. You cannot work safely around horses unless they are tied up. We tend to take liberties with horses and then wonder why accidents happen, even with our 'old faithfuls'. A ring should be placed at about 1.2m (4ft) high and preferably away from the door. A ring for a haynet should be about 1.8m (6ft) high ideally, but this may mean that you cannot reach it. It is difficult to site this ring, as an empty haynet will drop about 0.6m (2ft) and horses easily get caught up in them. Modern haynets are nearly all nylon, that does not break, so they should be tied to string and *removed* when empty. You may find it advantagous to have some tie-up rings outside the stable as well.

Hay racks When high enough to be safe (**fig. 7a**), these tend to be so high that seed and dust fall into the horse's eyes and nostrils.

Mangers Fixed mangers should be at chest height to the horse, and fitted flush to a corner. Care must be taken that the horse cannot get trapped underneath them, and that they are shaped so that the horse will not bang his knees if he paws whilst eating.

They must be easy to clean but not easy for the horse to remove and play with. It is a good idea to site them at the front of the box, so that you don't have to dodge a hungry horse every meal-time. It is possible to have flaps on the outside of the box that you open and tip the feed through.

A disadvantage of fixed mangers is that they are at the perfect height for the horse to crib bite them.

Removable managers come in different forms, but the two most common are the type that clip on the door, or durable feed bowls that you place on the ground. Certainly, feeding on the floor is more natural to the horse; saliva will flow more freely and the horse will eat more slowly, but problems with tipping the food out can occur, so a system such as putting the bowls in car tyres may be necessary.

Electric light It is important that you site the light correctly so that it is out of the reach of the horse, but gives maximum light. The light fitting itself should be waterproof, with toughened glass and a protective mesh covering. Switches should be outside the box, within easy reach for you, but not the horses. There must be no exposed cable in the box.

Automatic water bowls This system definitely is a time-saver. It is possible to have meters fitted that monitor how much a horse drinks, and taps so that you can turn the supply off should you wish. Freezing pipes are a major problem, but these can be lagged and a heat wire passed along the pipe that is thermostatically controlled. This is all very expensive, but definitely worthwhile in a large yard. The water bowls must be checked and scrubbed daily just as water buckets should be.

Water buckets These are some people's preference. They make it very easy to monitor how much or little a horse is drinking, but the disadvantage is that

horses tend to knock buckets over or knock bedding into them. It is possible to buy fixtures for buckets, but these are potentially dangerous, as your horse may easily get a leg through them.

Fire precautions

As already mentioned, it is important that in a barn system you have more than one exit (**fig. 8**). For any type of yard it is important that you have a fire drill. This should be displayed on a large sign in a central position in the yard. Fire notices should be around the yard, stating where the nearest telephone is and how to raise the alarm. Above the telephone there should be clear directions to give the fire service. 'No Smoking' signs should be placed strategically around the yard.

Extinguishers There are many different types, but it is generally best to have the foam type, as they can be used safely on both electrical and non-electrical fires.

Fire and smoke alarms Smoke alarms are particularly important in a barn system, where smoke can fill the whole building quickly. In large yards you will need several fire alarms.

SUMMARY

- Stables must be designed to create a healthy environment for the horse.
- The design must incorporate safety features.
- A well-designed yard will reduce labour and be more pleasant to work in.

4
BEDDING

4
BEDDING

When creating a healthy environment for the stabled horse, one of the most important factors is creating a dust-free atmosphere – more or less an impossible task. Yet many horses suffer from some form of respiratory problem, and most such problems go undetected until later life, or until the horse is asked to work under stress in competitions. The horse's lung capacity is comparatively large compared with other mammals, but the respiratory tract, from the throat down to the lungs, is extremely sensitive. Any irritation will result in coughing as this is the natural defence reflex. The bedding that we use is a major factor in the management and health of the horse, and to understand its importance it will help to study how the horse's respiratory system works.

The Respiratory System

Its major functions are to supply oxygen to the body, and to remove carbon dioxide (**fig. 9**).

The passage of air

Nostrils Air is taken in through the nostrils, which the horse can easily enlarge by dilating them should he need to take in more air when exerted. The air passes into the nasal cavities (**fig. 10**).

Nasal cavities These two cavities are separated from each other by the median cartilage, and from the mouth by the hard and soft palate. They are lined with vascular mucous membranes that warm and moisten the air. The sinuses open into the nasal cavity. The sinuses are a series of air-filled compartments joined together. The air then passes into the pharynx.

Pharynx The air passes into the nasopharynx. Both air and food pass through the pharynx, so it is divided into two sections (nasopharynx and oropharynx) by a sheet of muscle called the soft palate, which the trachea passes through. Unless the horse is swallowing the pharyngeal muscles will be relaxed, so the larynx and the epiglottis will be open, allowing air down the trachea (see Chapter 7).

Larynx This air passage connects the pharynx with the trachea, and is overhung by a protective piece of cartilage, the epiglottis. It helps to regulate inspiration and expiration, opening fully when the horse is galloping. It also acts as a trap, preventing foreign objects from entering the trachea.

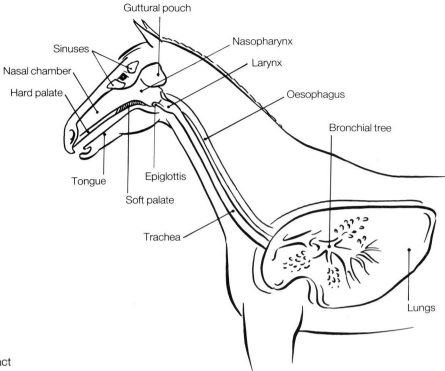

Fig. 9 The respiratory tract

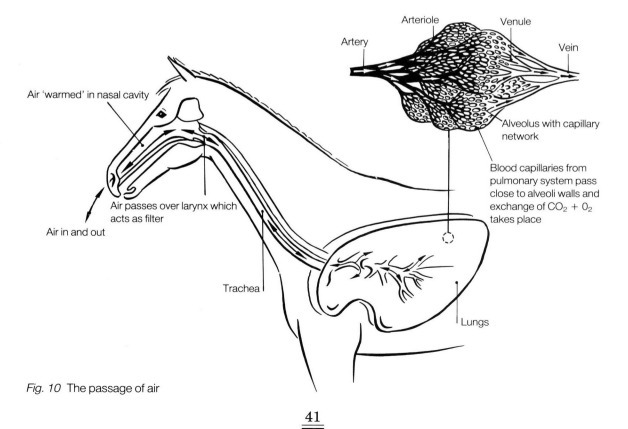

Fig. 10 The passage of air

Trachea The trachea is a long tube strengthened by 'C'-shaped rings of cartilage. Mucous membrane lines the trachea, and microscopic hairs called cilia help catch and expel dust and other solid particles, by sweeping them up towards the throat, from where they can be coughed out or swallowed. The trachea divides in the chest into two bronchi, one entering each lung.

Lungs In each lung, the bronchus branches into smaller bronchi and then into bronchioles. The lungs are enveloped by a membrane called the pleura.

Bronchioles These branch into alveolar ducts which run into alveolar sacs, containing many alveoli. Each alveolus is a blind sac.

Alveolus Blood capillaries from the pulmonary vascular system envelop the alveolar walls, and the exchange of oxygen and carbon dioxide takes place across their single cell thick walls. The expired air then travels the same journey in reverse.

The mechanics of respiration

The breathing rate is controlled by the amount of carbon dioxide in the arteries passing through the brain and other sensory areas. If the concentration of carbon dioxide in the blood is high, the breathing rate will increase. Carbon dioxide is created by the breakdown of nutrients, mainly carbohydrates, to produce energy for all cellular activities that require it, and high amounts of energy are produced in the muscle cells as the horse works.

Diaphragm This strong, flat, dome-shaped muscle is attached to the sternal (true) ribs. It draws back to lower the air pressure in the lungs, thus drawing air in.

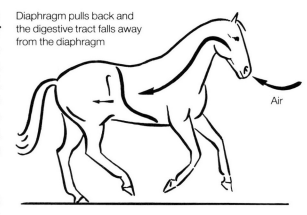

Diaphragm pulls back and the digestive tract falls away from the diaphragm

Air

Fig. 11 Diaphragm inhaling

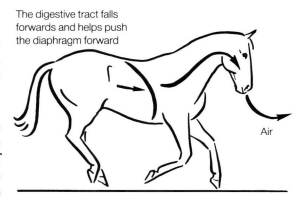

The digestive tract falls forwards and helps push the diaphragm forward

Air

Fig. 12 Diaphragm exhaling

It then relaxes and pushes forward to increase the air pressure and force the air out. Because of the close proximity of the stomach and intestines, the horse should not be worked at speed after feeding. In canter the breathing locks into the stride. The rise and fall of the canter/gallop enables the horse to inhale as he rises and his abdominal contents fall away from the diaphragm (**fig. 11**); and exhale as he lowers and his abdominal contents fall towards the diaphragm (**fig. 12**).

The effects of dust and spores

Although the respiratory system will cope with some dust and spores, if the concentration is too great, they will enter the alveoli and cause an allergic reaction in

some horses and excessive mucous production, thus narrowing and ultimately blocking some of the airways. This will cause the horse's performance to suffer when worked, as he will not be able to inhale enough oxygen, which is used to create energy in the muscles. Coughing is one of the first clinical signs.

Another problem that can occur is an allergic reaction to certain chemicals, a particular problem with some shavings that come from trees sprayed to encourage growth.

Choosing the best quality bedding will help to minimize the dust and spores, and it is possible to buy bedding that is guaranteed dust-free.

Bedding

The main reason for bedding is to encourage the horse to lie down and rest without injuring himself on the hard floor and walls. Many geldings or stallions will not stale on a hard surface such as concrete, as they do not like to splash themselves. If bedding is used in the correct quantity, it will also cut out draughts when the horse lies down, as it should raise him higher than the bottom of the door. Good quality, dry bedding will also help to keep the horse clean.

Deciding which bedding to use

The first priority must be the horse's own requirements, but generally bedding should be clean and dust-free (especially if your horse is allergic), dry, soft, and not injurious if eaten.

One problem that is a yard manager's constant nightmare is the disposal of manure. Straw manure can sometimes be sold to mushroom companies, but shavings and paper can be more of a problem although some garden centres will take it.

In some cases you may have to pay to have it taken away.

The availability of the bedding will affect the price. If it is scarce, it is expensive.

Straw This is the traditional bedding for horses. It does carry a risk of spores and fungi, even on the best quality. It probably is the most economical bedding and is the easiest to dispose of. If used it should be clean, shiny and not too fresh (older straw is more durable and less palatable). There are various types available:

Wheat Most commonly used, as it is thought to be the most durable and least palatable.

Barley Before modern harvesting, this was not used for horses, as the heads were not always removed. If horses did eat the heads, they were liable to get colic as barley heads are indigestible. Today this is not a problem, but horses sometimes pick up lice from barley straw.

Oat This can be used as fodder for field-kept ponies – so is not often used for bedding.

Rye Not commonly used as it is not easily available.

Shavings A good bedding if your horse tends to eat his bed. It is important that you control the intake of food with some horses, especially if they are competition horses on carefully formulated rations. It is not dust-free unless it has been passed through a dust extractor (ask your supplier about this). It does not have fungal spores, but can irritate some horses' skin if the wood that it is made from has been chemically treated. Although shavings can be expensive, proprietary brands are better, as the shavings should have been sifted for foreign objects. Disposal of the shavings muck heap can be difficult.

Sawdust This is not a good choice from the dust point of view. Some horses refuse to lie on it. It must be sorted for wood chips and splinters. It can be usefully mixed with shavings to help 'dry up' a bed.

Paper This is becoming more popular. It is completely dust-free and a must for horses with a respiratory disease. There are various brands of shredders on the market, which chop paper into different shapes. Some people worry about the newsprint ink, but this is not a problem as it is vegetable-based. However, people often make the mistake of putting a horse on paper to aid an allergy, only to have the horse next door on straw. Spores travel long distances, so to create a reasonably dust-free environment you must have the whole yard on paper, or other such materials. The only drawback with paper is its disposal.

Peat The main advantage of peat moss is that it is very absorbent. Sphagnum peat can absorb up to ten times its own weight in liquid. It is very expensive and often makes a damp bedding, as it tends to absorb even the moisture from the air. It was used for horses with respiratory problems, but has now been replaced by paper.

Management of bedding

Storage It is important that the bedding is kept dry. Mould will cause harm to the horse and could mean that large amounts of bedding are wasted. When storing in large quantities, you must also consider the problems of vermin. Rats will nest in the bedding, and this carries health risks as it is possible to catch leptospirosis (Weil's disease) from their urine. So when stacking your bedding,

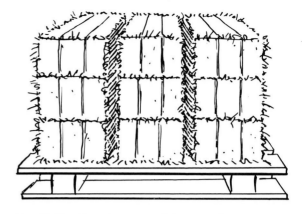

Fig. 13 Stacking straw on pallets correctly

put down poison. Bedding should be stacked off the ground on pallets, and if stacking straw it is a good idea to stack the bottom row on their sides as rats will be less likely to chew through the strings (**fig. 13**).

Handling Humans suffer from allergies too. You should wear a mask if handling straw or other dusty materials. It is also a good idea to wear gloves to minimize the risk of catching Weil's disease. This disease is very similar to hepatitis and can be serious.

If you are handling heavy weights, lift them correctly and do not carry them for long distances (**fig. 14**).

Mucking out There are three main systems:

Complete muck-out This is when all the soiled bedding is removed and the unsoiled bedding moved right back against the sides of the box. The floor should be swept and fresh bedding added. If possible, the floor should be given time to dry. Some people will have a thinner 'day bed' and then bed down with more bedding in the evening. This can be useful with straw beds, as horses tend to eat it during the day. Thickness of the bed is a personal preference (**7**). If it is too thick, it

is difficult to manage, too thin and the horse may suffer injuries such as capped hocks or elbows. A good guide is to drop a fork, prongs down, onto the bed. You should not hit the floor.

Semi-deep litter This is a particularly good method to use with shavings and paper. The droppings and the worst of the wet bedding is removed each day, and the bedding is topped up as necessary.

Any type of deep-litter system only really works if the box is a decent size. Deep-litter systems will not save on bedding, but will save on time. If the box is small, the bed tends to become sodden and then you will use more bedding than if you were on complete muck-out.

Deep litter The box must be large and well ventilated. With this system, you remove only the droppings. You must keep adding plenty of bedding for the first few weeks, until you have a firm base. You have to watch that the bed does not build up too high and you may have to remove it if it starts to smell. Ammonia is produced from the urine and the decaying matter. It is caustic and unhealthy for the horse.

7 A stable 'set fair' – always use plenty of bedding

Fig. 14 Lifting heavy weights correctly, with a straight back

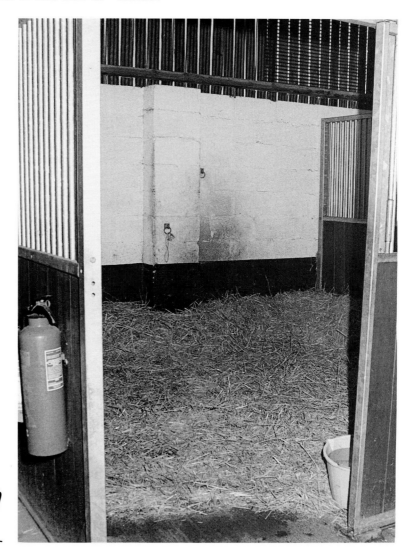

Banking the bed To stop horses getting stuck against the wall (cast), bank the bedding around the edge of the box. (Although this may help, most horses that are prone to getting cast will do so anyway.) For the banks to be effective they have to be fairly solid and thick. It is better to run a ridge around the inside of the stable wall about 1m (3ft 6in) from the ground, for the horse to push against with his hooves should he get cast. Banks help to cut out draughts, too.

SAFETY RULES

- Always tie the horse up when working in the stable; never take him for granted **(8)**.
- Always fork away from the horse. Even your 'old faithful' can be unpredictable **(8)**.
- If using a wheelbarrow, do not have the handles into the box, as the horse may catch himself on them **(8)**.
- If handling a nervous or unpredictable horse do not muck out with the door open. Put the muck in the doorway and fork it into the wheelbarrow when you have finished.
- Never leave tools lying around in the box.

---

8 Safety is important when mucking out

Muck heaps

There is a saying that 'the standard of a yard's stable management can be judged by the tidiness of the muck heap' **(9)**.

However, this often means that people spend hours on the muck heap and little time on anything else. It is true that building a muck heap properly is the best way to encourage the muck to rot quickly, and enables you to store the muck more effectively.

It is best to have an area that is enclosed on three sides by a high wall. The muck should be properly packed down, with the front forked straight for a good appearance.

SUMMARY

- Dust-free bedding is healthier for the horse, as the respiratory tract is very sensitive.
- Use good quality, dry bedding, which will also keep the horse clean.
- Whichever system you choose you must use plenty of bedding.
- Handle the horse and equipment safely.

9 A tidy muck heap

Part 2
CARE AND MANAGEMENT

5
THE HEALTHY HORSE

To recognize when a horse is unwell, you must recognize the signs of health. Observation is of paramount importance when caring for the horse, and information given by the handler will aid a veterinary surgeon's diagnosis if the horse is unwell. All horses are individuals, and just noticing a change of mood in the horse may tell you that all is not well.

Along with any physical disease that the horse may suffer from, we must also consider the psychological problems that may cause a horse to be below par. Bad management, stress of work, poor training, change of environment, or just a change of routine can all have an effect on the horse. It is important that you investigate if you notice the slightest change and consult your veterinary surgeon if you think there is a problem.

Signs of Health

Physical condition

Alert expression This is the first and most obvious sign of health. Horses are naturally inquisitive. Does the horse acknowledge you? Does he seem interested in what is around him?

Respiration The normal respiratory rate of the horse is between eight and sixteen breaths per minute. If the horse is blowing, this could be a sign of pain. Also, if the respiration is laboured, this could mean there is some kind of respiratory disease.

Coughing is a sign of disease and is of concern. If the horse also has a temperature, it is a sign of a respiratory infection. Allergies will also make the horse cough, and if untreated, in time the horse may suffer a chronic respiratory problem that could render him unworkable.

Nostrils These should be kept clean, and the mucous membrane that lines them should be salmon pink in colour. Some discharge during or after work is normal, provided that the horse is not coughing as well. However, if there is discharge when the horse is in the stable, then it must not be ignored, particularly if it is foul-smelling.

A white discharge may indicate a dust allergy, whilst a yellow discharge indicates infection or disease, possibly of the respiratory system or the sinus cavities. A bloody discharge out of one nostril is usually not too serious, although your vet should be consulted. If it comes out of both nostrils, this may indicate haemorrhage from the lungs.

Eyes These should be clear, bright and shiny. If there is any pus discharge or inflammation, the vet should be consulted. It may be just a simple scratch to the eye, but it could be the start of a more serious còndition.

Stance The horse should stand on all four limbs. It is natural for a horse to rest a hind leg, but you should still move him to see if he will bear weight on it. If a horse is 'pointing' a foreleg forward, then you will have to investigate further, as

Fig. 15 Pointing a foreleg

Fig. 16 A horse looking 'tucked up'

this is not normal (**fig. 15**). Sometimes, horses will rest a diagonal hind and foreleg together. This can be a sign of back problems. If the horse is standing, looks dull and tucked up, possibly holding his tail in the air, this is a sign of pain or discomfort (**fig. 16**). Another sign of discomfort is if the horse is restless.

Coat The coat reflects the condition of the skin and the general health of the horse. It should be dry, flat and shiny. A dull coat is a sign of poor condition. If the coat is sweaty at rest, this is a sign of the horse having a temperature or being in pain.

Condition The amount of weight the horse is carrying is an important factor. No horse can be too big in condition, as long as he is not fat. Obesity is unhealthy; it overburdens the heart and limbs (**10**).

However, being thin does not mean that the horse is fit. A fit horse will be lean but well-muscled (**12**).

Appetite Horses will generally eagerly await and eat their feed (**11**). If the horse refuses to eat, it is a sure sign that he is out of sorts.

The stable

Bedding If the bedding is churned up, or badly disturbed, this is a sign that the horse has been restless (a sign of pain) or has been cast. Look around the walls for

(Below) **10** Obesity is unhealthy for the horse

(Top right) **11** A horse in good condition

(Bottom Right) **12** A fit horse will be lean and well-muscled

any signs of a struggle, i.e. scrape marks on the wall. Check the horse over and trot him up to see if he is sound.

Droppings The most obvious sign is the smell. Evil-smelling droppings are a sign of digestive problems. No droppings at all could mean that the horse is constipated, or, more seriously, that there is a blockage in the intestinal tract. Horses do sometimes eat their droppings; this is caused mainly by mineral deficiency. Diarrhoea can be serious. It may only be caused by an incorrect diet, but it is a symptom of more serious complaints. If it lasts more than a day, your veterinary surgeon should be consulted. Diarrhoea will also cause dehydration, which in itself is serious.

INVESTIGATING FURTHER

If any of the above does not seem normal, then you must investigate further. This will mean that should you call the vet you will be able to give a detailed account of the symptoms.

Temperature Take the temperature by placing a thermometer that has been lubricated with Vaseline (petroleum jelly), or another veterinary lubricant, in the rectum and holding it there for two minutes. The horse's normal temperature should be around 38°C or 101.5°F. Any rise of temperature could be a sign of infection, and the vet should be consulted. It is rare that the temperature will drop, but note that a drop in temperature is potentially fatal as the horse will suffer hypothermia.

Pulse The normal pulse is 36–40 beats per minute. A rapid pulse is a sign of pain. A shallow, fast pulse can be a sign of poisoning. Irregularity in the beat could signify a heart condition. The pulse may be taken in several ways. The best way is

to use a stethoscope, placing it on the left-hand side about 15cm (6in) from the elbow (**13**). Alternatively, you can feel the pulse of the facial artery where it crosses the lower jaw-bone (**14**). Do not take the pulse with your thumb, as this has a pulse of its own.

It is important to have a record of your horse's normal temperature, pulse and respiration, as the rates can vary between horses. When you know what is normal, you will also know what is abnormal.

(Opposite) **13** Taking the pulse with a stethoscope

(Below) **14** Taking the pulse at the facial artery

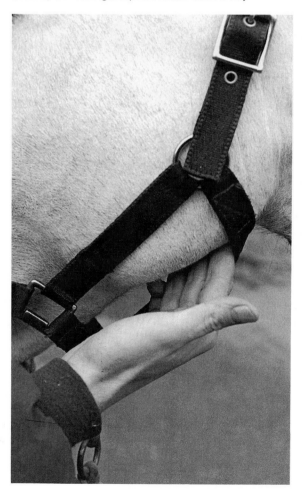

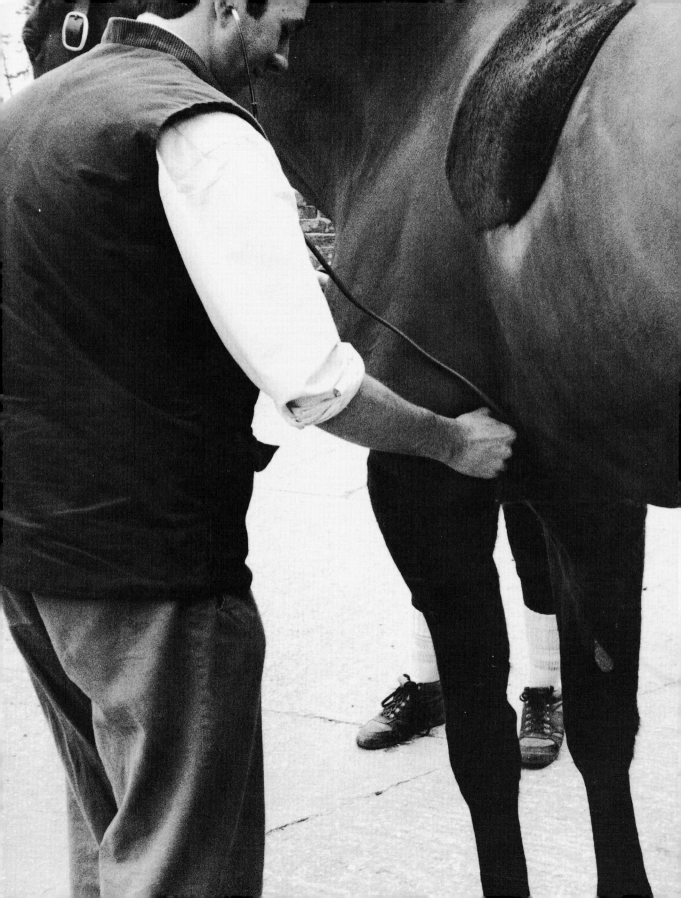

Mucous Membranes These change colour, depending on the health of the horse, and this is particularly true of the inner lining of the eyelids (15). Normally they should be salmon pink. Pale membranes may signify anaemia; yellow membranes may signify liver complaint; bright red membranes may signify fever; and brick-red membranes may signify blood poisoning.

Skin This should run smoothly and freely over the body. If the skin is tight and is slow to recoil when pinched, it is a sign that the horse is dehydrated (16). Dehydration, even in slight amounts, will affect performance. If the skin is in poor condition, then this reflects the general health of the horse. The skin can be affected by many diseases, not just those specific to the skin.

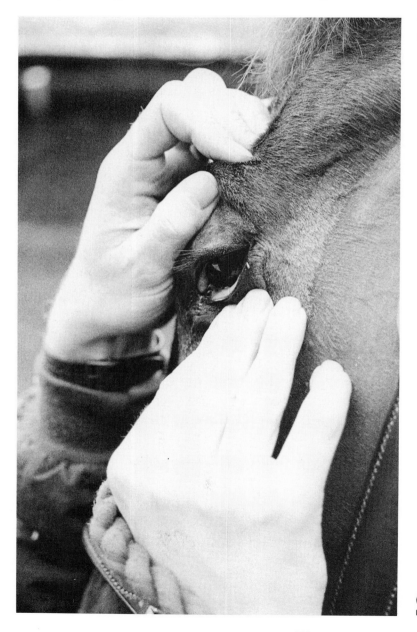

15 Examining the mucous membranes of the eye

(Opposite) **16** The pinch test is used to check for dehydration

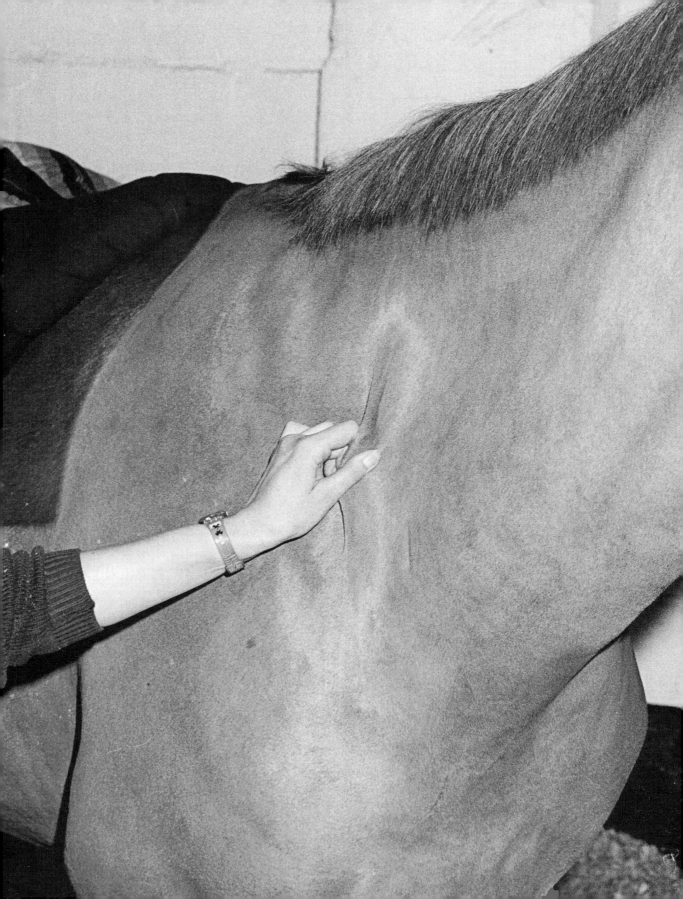

Legs and hooves The legs should be cold and clean. Any swelling, heat, or pain to touch will signify inflammation. The feet should be cool. If the horse is favouring a leg, particularly a foreleg, you should feel for pain, heat or swelling. If none is apparent, it is probable that the lameness is in the foot. In either case, you should see the horse move to see if he places his weight evenly on all four feet.

Urine This should be clear. Any discolouration signifies disorder or disease. It may be only a slight imbalance of feed, but it could be a more serious condition, such as a kidney infection.

Routine Health Care

Teeth

These should be rasped at least annually (**17**). With old horses, you may find that you need to have the teeth rasped more often. The back molars in particular, will wear sharp, and affect the way a horse eats, in some cases cutting the gums. This could cause loss of condition. Sharp teeth will also make it uncomfortable for a horse to accept the bit.

Vaccinations

In Great Britain there are three common vaccinations given to help the horse build up immunity. They work on the principle of injecting a treated, safe form of the disease, to stimulate the body into producing antibodies to fight it.

There are 'live' vaccines and 'dead' vaccines. Live vaccines contain a virus or bacteria that has been treated so as not to cause disease. This vaccine gives good immunity for a short period. Dead vaccines contain the strain of virus or bacteria that has been treated so that it is dead: they are only effective if given in a regular course of boosters.

Influenza (a dead vaccine) The horse will need a course of injections. The first two will be given 21–90 days apart and then the third injection 150–215 days later. Then a booster is given annually, although many veterinary surgeons recommend a booster every six to eight months to give better immunity.

Tetanus (a dead vaccine) A course of injections with the first two given three or four weeks apart and the third a year later. The horse will then require a booster only every other year.

Equine herpes (EHV–1) This is a virus that can cause abortion in breed stock. Vaccination is becoming more widespread. There are two types of vaccine, a dead vaccine for the abortion virus and a live vaccine for the respiratory version of the disease. The horse will have a course of two boosters followed by a further booster as often as every three months.

In the United States also horses are vaccinated for tetanus, influenza and EHV–1 (referred to as rhinopneumonitis). Horses may also be vaccinated against:

Eastern and Western Encephalomyelitis This disease causes paralysis. There are three strains of this virus: Eastern, Western and Venezuelan. As there is no specific treatment, vaccination is an important preventive measure. Two doses of the vaccine are given ten days apart in the early spring, then the horse will be revaccinated annually.

Rabies This fatal virus affects the central nervous system. It is transmitted by saliva, usually by bites from affected animals. It is possible to vaccinate, although

this is more common with dogs or cats. A booster is given annually.

Potomac Horse Fever This can cause paralysis. An effective vaccination programme has yet to be developed. Opinions vary, so it is wise to seek the advice of your own vet.

Strangles This is a respiratory disease caused by the bacteria streptococcus equi. Vaccination is possible, although it is not long-lasting. However, it may reduce the severity of the disease.

Worming Parasites live and thrive off another animal. The degree of damage can vary, but generally the parasite will thrive and its host will suffer (**fig. 17**). As the horse grows older, it will develop immunity to some parasites, but young horses will be susceptible to damage.

Good pasture management will help to reduce the worm burden. Fields should be regularly topped, as the larvae can crawl up long stems to re-infect the horse. Cross-grazing with sheep or cattle will help, as the worms cannot survive these animals' intestinal tracts. Remove drop-

17 Rasping the teeth, using a gag

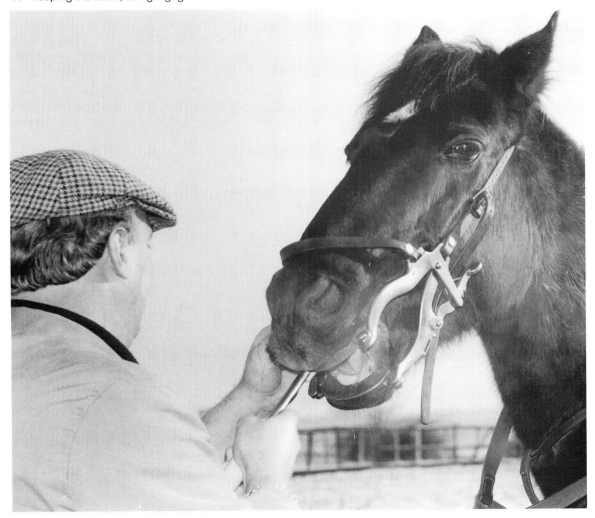

pings from pasture at least twice a week in summer when the larvae are developing rapidly. On less intensively grazed land, regular harrowing, especially in summer, will help, as the sun will dry up and kill some of the larvae. The most important treatment is a regular worming programme using anthelmintics. These are most commonly given orally in a powder or paste form. In severe cases, the vet may administer them by stomach tube.

All horses must follow a strict worming programme. The grass-kept horse will need worming at least every six weeks, especially during the spring and summer when the larvae are developing rapidly. During the winter, the horse should be specifically wormed for stomach bots as they are developing at this time in the horse's stomach. The stabled horse will not be exposed to worms to the same extent as the grass-kept horse, but if the horse is turned out at all, he may be invaded by worms, so will need to be wormed as often as the grass-kept horse. Some strains of worm have become immune to some anthelmintics, but a powerful drug called ivermectin is effective at killing most endoparasites. This drug circulates in the blood stream, so will also kill the migrating larvae. When using wormers, you should consult your vet as to the best type for your horse.

There are many different types of parasite, but the most common that we protect the horse against are the ones that live and develop in the intestinal tract. These are called endoparasites. These are:

Red worms (Strongyles) The most harmful round worms; they can cause death. They are about ½in (13mm) long and feed on the lining of the intestine. The larvae penetrate the gut wall and migrate through the arteries, liver and other tissues. This can cause thrombosis or haemorrhage, which in turn can lead to

Fig. 17 Life cycle of worms

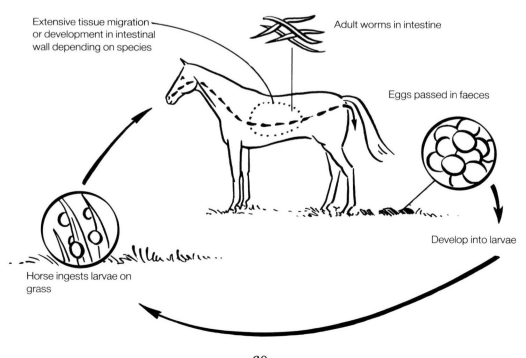

Extensive tissue migration or development in intestinal wall depending on species

Adult worms in intestine

Eggs passed in faeces

Develop into larvae

Horse ingests larvae on grass

tissue death. Such cases are usually fatal. Red worms account for about 90 per cent of eggs passed by the horse.

White worms (Ascarids) These round worms can eventually travel to the lungs, where they break through the blood vessels and migrate up the trachea, they are then coughed up and swallowed, maturing in the intestine into egg-laying adults. While not such a problem in adult horses, foals can suffer from infestation.

Pin or thread worms (Oxyuris) These roundworms live in the hind gut. The female lays her eggs in the horse's anus, making the horse itch and rub his tail.

Tape worms (flatworms) These can grow up to 2–3ft (60–75cm) long. They live in the intestines, and will cause the horse's condition to suffer.

Stomach bots (Gastrophilus) The yellow eggs of the gadfly are found on the horse's legs in summer. The horse licks the larvae off the coat. These bury themselves in the lining of the mouth and then migrate to the stomach. Here they attach themselves to the stomach wall. In the spring they pass out in the horse's droppings and hatch into flies. Removal of the eggs with a bot knife will help reduce infestation.

SUMMARY

- Observation is of paramount importance when caring for horses.
- Recognize the general signs of health.
- Know what is normal for your horse.
- Follow routine treatments to maintain health.

6

CARING FOR THE SICK OR INJURED HORSE

6

CARING FOR THE SICK OR INJURED HORSE

Correct care of the sick or injured horse will prevent the condition from worsening and aid his speedy recovery. Most treatments will be under veterinary supervision. Some conditions may require that the horse is isolated, particularly if the condition is contagious (spread by contact) or infectious (spread by air, water, etc.). Many conditions can be infectious and contagious. Complete hygenic isolation is only really possible by removing the horse to another premises. It is possible, however, to greatly reduce the spread of disease by having a separate isolation area and following a strict isolation procedure. This probably will not be practical for small yards, but is important on large yards, particularly those that have horses coming in from elsewhere, as on arrival they should be placed in isolation, and kept there for at least three weeks. The isolation area should be built away from the main stables, preferably down wind.

Isolation Stables

- These should be built of brick or concrete so that they can be disinfected easily. Wood can harbour disease for a considerable time.

- Each stable should be about 4.3 × 4.3m (14 × 14ft). This will help give the horse more ventilation. As with all stables, good ventilation is vital, but there must be no draughts.

- It must be possible to darken the box completely. This is sometimes necessary if the horse has eye injuries or is suffering from a nervous disease.

- Some form of heating system can be useful, particularly with very sick horses during cold weather. Infra-red lamps are probably the best form of heating. These should be covered, and set well out of the reach of the horse. These can also be used for strained muscles or for older, stiffer horses before exercise to warm up the muscles.

- There should be an area in which to store all equipment, feed and bedding to be used for horses in isolation. They must have their own mucking-out tools, grooming kits, etc. Nothing should go back to the main yard, or be used on another horse until it has been disinfected.

- If the isolation area is not near a house, there should be somewhere for the attendant to stay if constant supervision is required. It may be necessary to have some form of communication, such as a telephone.

- A separate muck heap is essential.
- There should be a small paddock area adjoining the stables for the horse to graze during recuperation.

Isolation procedure

- One person should look after the diseased horse and have no contact with the main yard or horses on it, unless he or she has washed thoroughly and changed clothing.
- Hands should be washed after handling the isolated horse.
- A disinfectant foot-bath should be placed at the entrance to the isolation area for people to wash their boots when entering and leaving the area.
- A sign should be placed at the entrance of the isolation area stating 'Isolation Area. Please Do Not Enter'.
- All equipment that is used with the isolated horse should be disinfected afterwards. The isolation area should have its own equipment, that is not used on the main yard.
- All soiled bedding should be placed on a separate muck heap to that of the main yard, and burned.

Sick nursing

Good nursing is of primary importance when treating disease. Any treatment prescribed by the vet should be strictly adhered too. Observation is important; daily records of the sick horse's health should be kept, and any changes reported to the vet. It is a good idea to keep a record of the vet's visits and any drugs, etc. used, as this will help you check against the final bill.

Medication This will be prescribed by the vet and a record should be kept of any drug administration. It is an offence for anyone to prescribe drugs if they are not a qualified veterinary surgeon. Medication may be given in the horse's feed, water, or by injection. Injections take three main forms:

Intravenous This will be done by the vet when rapid onset of a drug is required. The drug is normally injected into the jugular vein in the neck.

Intramuscular This is used for prolonged treatments. Some vets will instruct experienced people to inject the horse this way themselves. The injections are given into any large areas of muscle, usually on the neck, hindquarters or chest.

Subcutaneous This is when the drug or fluid is injected into a flap of skin, usually on the neck, where the skin is loose.

Warmth The sick horse will not be able to both fight disease and keep sufficently warm. If rugs are used, they should be lightweight and warm for comfort. Thermal rugs are particularly good. It may be necessary, in cold weather, to apply stable bandages. In cold weather, especially with debilitating disease, infra-red heating can be useful (see above).

Feeding The diet must be cut down and only contain the required nutrients to combat disease and maintain condition. Vitamins and minerals are important, and some protein should be given. Feeds should be appetizing and nutritious. Energy-giving foods with high amounts of carbohydrates should not be fed as the horse will not be working. Bran mashes do not provide sufficient nutrition for the sick horse. Horses with a respiratory disease will have to be fed Haylage (see Chapter 7), or well-soaked hay. With respiratory disease, it is a good idea to feed on the ground to help drain any mucous. All feed bowls, haynets and utensils should be regularly disinfected.

Water The amount that the horse drinks should be carefully monitored. Dehydration is very serious. A fresh, constant supply of water should be provided. Any buckets used should be regularly disinfected.

Bedding Paper is the best bedding for any respiratory disorder. With very sick horses, you may need to deep litter the box so as not to disturb the horse to much.

Grooming If possible, gentle grooming will make the horse feel better as it stimulates circulation. Eyes, nose and dock should be sponged regularly, particularly if there is a lot of discharge. Use a separate grooming kit for the sick horse and disinfect it between horses.

Convalescence

After most diseases, particularly those involving the respiratory system, a period of convalescence will be required. This will probably be spent in the field, as the natural environment is the best way of aiding recovery. Bringing the horse back into work too soon could cause a relapse.

Simple Medical Treatments

Poulticing

A poultice is used to reduce heat, pain, swelling and infection. They can be applied hot or cold. They should be changed every eight to 12 hours and applications should not continue for more than three days without consulting your vet, as you may start to draw out the healthy tissue, which will result in excess scar tissue. With bad infections, poulticing alone will not be enough, the horse will probably require antibiotics as well. There are a number of ready-prepared poultices on the market. These are quick and convenient to use as the dressing is impregnated with the drawing agent. Traditionally, kaolin paste (China clay), Epsom salts (magnesium sulphate) and boracic powder have been used. Open wounds over a joint should not be poulticed, unless the vet prescribes so, as it could draw out the joint oil.

Procedure
- Clean the area thoroughly.
- If a wound, trim the hair around it. If it is a puncture to the sole of the hoof, it may need to be enlarged by your farrier.
- Place gauze over the area. With a wound, it is a good idea to put Vaseline (petroleum jelly) on the area to stop the dressing sticking.
- Place the dressing with the drawing agent against the area.
- Cover with polythene, so that the poultice draws from the area only. The polythene will also keep the dressing clean and keep some heat in.
- Bandage in place, using plenty of padding for comfort.

Tubbing

This is useful for injuries to the foot, especially before poulticing (18). Tubbing will increase blood flow to the area and help draw out infection. It is only beneficial if it is done several times a day, and for at least 20 minutes.

Procedure
- Place boiling water in a plastic or rubber bowl. Buckets tend to be a little narrow and the horse will tip them over easily.
- Add two handfuls of Epsom salts to act as a drawing agent.
- Add cold water to bring the temperature to 'hand hot'.

- Scrub the horse's foot clean, grease the heel area and place in the bowl.

Fomentations

These are used to apply heat to areas that are difficult to bandage. Fomentations can be useful for relieving bruising, or sore muscles. Like tubbing, this is only beneficial if done several times a day and for at least 20 minutes.

Procedure
- Prepare the water as for tubbing.
- Place a thick towel into the water and wring it out.
- Fold the towel to retain the heat and place on the area.
- Try and ensure that the heat is kept fairly even for the whole treatment.

18 Tubbing a foot

Cold hosing

This is useful to reduce the acute inflamation caused by haemorrhage (bruising), for reducing profuse bleeding, and for cleaning wounds (19). The 'cold' reduces the blood flow by causing the vessels to constrict. Treatment is most effective if done for just five or ten minutes, several times a day. If you apply cold to areas for long periods, it will actually increase blood flow, as the body will increase the circulation to warm the area.

Procedure

- If hosing a leg, grease the heel to prevent the skin cracking.
- Introduce the hose to the leg gradually and run the water gently.
- Dry the area thoroughly when finished.

It is possible to buy 'Aqua-Boots' which have a ring of mini-hoses, fed from a normal hose, that run water down the horse's lower leg.

19 Cold hosing a leg

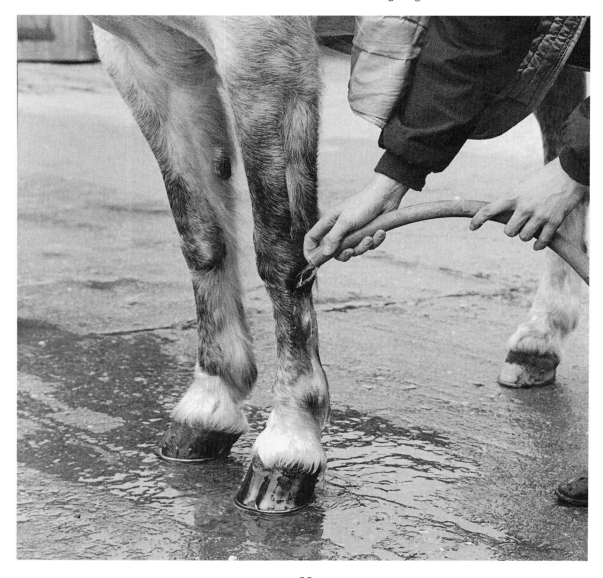

Massage

This can be a very effective treatment and therapy for muscle damage or strain. It can also help to disperse fluid, providing that the area is not too painful to massage. Hand-massage will relieve only superficial injury. Deeper injuries may require the use of specialist machines such as Ultra Sonic and Faradic.

Wounds

There are four main types of wound:

Lacerated or torn This wound can be difficult to treat as infection often develops under a flap of skin. Unless a blood vessel has been cut as well, the bleeding is minimal.

Incised or clean cut This wound will often bleed profusely due to vessels having been cut. This can be potentially fatal if an artery has been cut, in which case the blood will come out in bright red spurts. Control the bleeding by applying direct pressure to the wound with a pad. Tourniquets should not be used as they will cut off the blood supply to the healthy tissue around the wound. It is important that you do not remove the pad until the vet arrives, to give the blood time to form a seal.

With major arterial bleeding you must resort to whatever means you can to control the bleeding, even if this means that you use a tourniquet. A tourniquet should be applied between the wound and the heart over the major artery that supplies the area. Wrap a small pebble in a large handkerchief or length of cloth and place the pebble over the artery. Pull the ends of the handkerchief together and tie a length of wood into the knot. Turn the length of wood to tighten the tourniquet until the blood flow is reduced. A tourniquet must not be applied for more than 15 minutes without loosening, as the tourniquet will also restrict the flow of blood to the healthy tissue that surrounds the wound. The vet will stitch this type of wound.

Contused, or bruised The important thing with this type of wound is to stop the haemorrhaging. First cold hose, and then apply a poultice to stimulate healing.

Puncture The problem with this type of wound is that it is deeper than it is wide, so infection is common. Poulticing is the most effective treatment as it will encourage the wound to heal from the inside.

General treatment of wounds to prevent infection

Most invading germs that cause infection thrive in anaerobic (without oxygen) conditions. Incorrect treatment or neglect of even minor wounds can lead to serious infection.

Procedure

- Clean the wound by hosing or swabbing with sterile cotton wool. Use a clean piece for each swab to prevent re-infecting the wound.
- Trim hair and dead skin around the wound where possible.
- If the vet is to see the wound, only treat with a mild antiseptic, such as saline solution (4g (0.14oz) of salt to 1l (0.25-gal) of water) or diluted hydrogen peroxide (20 vol 6 per cent B.P.). The vet may wish to administer antibiotics. Strong antiseptics should not be used as they will kill off the 'good germs', that are fighting the infection, as well as the 'bad'. Otherwise, apply antiseptic powder.
- Where possible, keep the wound open to the air as this will help prevent anaerobic infection. Syringing the wound with diluted hydrogen peroxide helps to get oxygen into the wound.

- Unless the wound looks as if it may be becoming infected, let it heal and just regularly re-apply antiseptic powder.

All wounded horses must be vaccinated for tetanus. If in doubt, call the vet.

Bandaging

Surgical bandaging This can be useful to control swelling and hold dressings in place. Modern, self-adhesive bandages have rendered some of the traditional methods redundant. However, surgical bandages can be particularly useful when pressure is required to an area. There are specialist bandages on the market that have medical or therapeutic properties.

Stable bandages Some horses suffer from 'filled legs' when stabled. This is due to the lymphatic system not being able to remove the excess fluid that has seeped through its vessel walls. This seeping of fluid is caused by excessive protein in the lymph, usually indicating an inbalanced diet. Bandaging will improve the circulation and may help to reduce the filling.

Pressure bandage This is used in conjunction with an ice pack to control haemorraghing in cases such as tendon or ligament strain (**fig. 18**). Plenty of padding must be applied and held in place by a stable bandage. Over this you apply a slightly elasticated bandage to supply the pressure. They should be changed every two hours and the leg rubbed to stimulate circulation.

Joint or figure-of-eight bandage This is used to keep dressings in place. It is best to use self-adhesive bandages as others tend to slip (**fig. 19**). When bandaging the front leg, care should be taken not to bandage over the accessory carpal (pisiform) at the back of the knee, as you may dislodge it (**fig. 20 and 21**).

Fig. 18 Fitting a pressure bandage

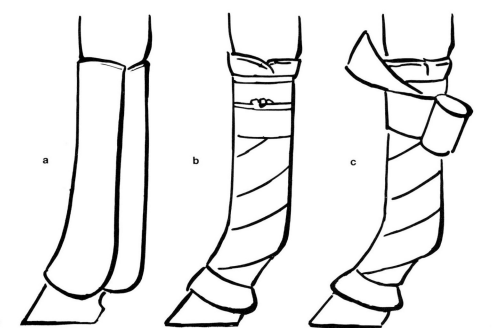

a Place plenty of padding around leg

b Secure padding with stable bandage

c Apply pressure with slightly elasticated bandage

Fig. 19 Fitting a hock bandage

a Place plenty of padding around joint. Applying stable bandage helps stop the main bandage slipping

b Bandage in place with a self adhesive or slightly elasticated bandage

c Bandage forms figure-of-eight that crosses on one side of joint

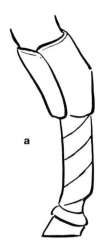
a

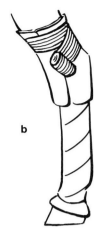
b

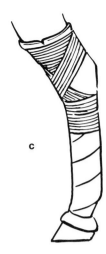
c

Fig. 20 Fitting a knee bandage

a Place plenty of padding around joint

b Bandage in place with self adhesive or slightly elasticated bandage

c Bandage forms figure-of-eight. Be careful not to put pressure on pisiform bone

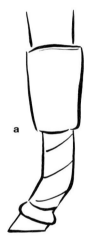
a

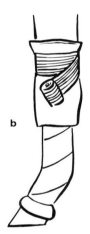
b

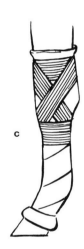
c

Fig. 21 Bandaging the front of the knee

The front of the knee can be bandaged if pressure is required

SUMMARY

- Isolation will reduce the spread of disease.
- Correct nursing of the sick horse will aid recovery.
- Keep accurate records of health and sickness, in case the vet requires them.
- Ensure all wounds are treated correctly to prevent infection.

7
FEEDING A
BALANCED DIET

7
FEEDING A BALANCED DIET

Feeding the horse is becoming an increasingly scientific activity. A greater knowledge of how the horse's digestive system breaks down food to obtain nutrients, and how the horse's physiology adapts to stress has led us to monitor our horses' diets more carefully.

Modern developments mean that many of us now buy feeds that have been compounded and 'balanced'. Feed is heat-treated in different ways to make it more digestible; and the utilization of nutrients can be monitored by blood tests.

Feeding the balanced diet demands that one provides the correct quantities of diet constituents, this in turn is governed by the size, type, breed, and work being done by the horse. Also, the conditions in which the horse is kept, his age, and temperament must be considered. Therefore, although the science is important, we still should feed the horse we see, handle and exercise.

The Horse's Digestive System

Ingestion – the intake of food (**fig. 22**).

Prehension The horse grasps the food with his muscular lips, and cuts up the food with his incisors.

Mastication The horse grinds up the food with his molars and mixes it with saliva. Saliva is an alkaline fluid which lubricates the food, making it easier to swallow and 'aerates' it, making it easier to digest. The food is formed into a bolus that is moved to the back of the throat by the molars.

Swallowing The strong muscular action of the tongue, pushing the food into the oropharynx, causes the pharyngeal muscles to contract (**fig. 23**). This lifts the soft palate, lowers the larynx to shut off the trachea with the epiglottis, and the food is pushed into the oesophagus.

Oesophagus This is about 4ft (120cm) long and is lined with muscle. It runs down between the two lungs and into the stomach. Food is passed along the oesophagus by a wave-like muscular motion, called 'peristalsis'. This can be seen by watching the lower neck on the left hand side whilst the horse eats or drinks.

Digestion and absorption of nutrients

The stomach This is comparatively small, and can hold about 3gal (11l). Food enters through the cardiac sphincter, one-way muscular valve. The food is churned

74

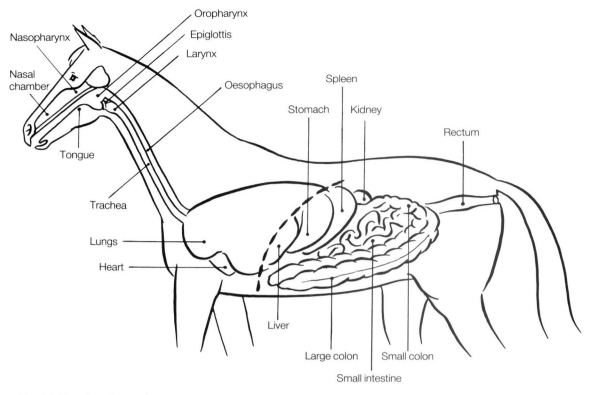

Fig. 22 The digestive system

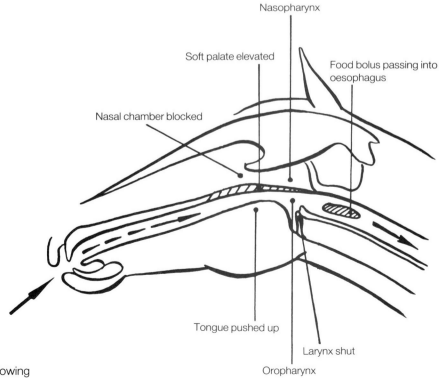

Fig. 23 The action of swallowing

and mixed with the gastric juices, which are secreted by the fundic glands. These juices contain the enzymes: rennin (a curdling enzyme), lipase (breaks down fats) and pepsin (breaks down proteins). These enzymes are activated by hydrochloric acid, which is also secreted in the stomach. The stomach is lined with mucous membrane to protect it from the acid. The food (as acid 'chyme') passes into the small intestine through the pyloric sphincter. Food will stay in the stomach for up to 1½ hours before moving on to the intestines.

Small intestine This is divided into three sections:

Duodenum Food is further broken down here by duodenal secretions, which are alkaline and thus neutralize the acid chyme. Duodenal secretions include bile, which emulsifies fats and prepares them for further absorption. Pancreatic juice in the duodenum breaks down starch into simple sugars; breaks down protein into amino acids; and further breaks down fats.

Jejunum and ileum The food passes along by peristalsis. The intestines are lined with small, finger-like projections, called 'villi', which increase the surface area and thus greatly increase the absorption capacity. The simple sugars, minerals, vitamins and amino acids are absorbed through the intestinal wall, into the bloodstream. The remaining food products then pass into the large intestine.

Large intestine This contains the caecum, the colon and the rectum.

The caecum This acts as a collecting chamber for the:

Large colon In the caecum and large colon live bacteria or 'gut flora'. These

form cellulase which breaks down cellulose and in doing so manufacture volatile fatty acids, Vitamin B_{12} and Vitamin C. These gut flora are very sensitive to change, so a sudden change in diet could wipe them out, causing imbalances and the possible production of toxins.

The waste products then pass into the small colon and rectum.

Small colon and rectum Here water and minerals are absorbed as necessary. Waste is formed into dung and excreted through the anus. It takes up to two to three days for food to pass through the intestinal tract (**fig. 24**).

Formulating a Ration

The most important thing to remember when formulating a ration for a horse, is that he is a 'trickle' feeder. In nature he will graze and wander, his stomach two-thirds full and his intestine slowly breaking down the cellulose of the grass. Therefore, he should be fed small amounts often and, most importantly, plenty of roughage. No horse can be too big in condition, as long as he isn't fat. Water is most essential as besides its important metabolic function, it is vital for digestion.

Choice of feedstuffs

All natural feedstuffs are made up of six basic constituents: proteins, carbohydrates, fats and oils, vitamins and minerals. These are present in varying amounts, so the nutritional values of different feedstuffs will differ. Concentrates contain these constituents in a concentrated form, particularly carbohydrates and proteins, so are fed in small amounts.

Proteins These are used for the repair of body cells, and for growth. They can be stored in the body in an active form such

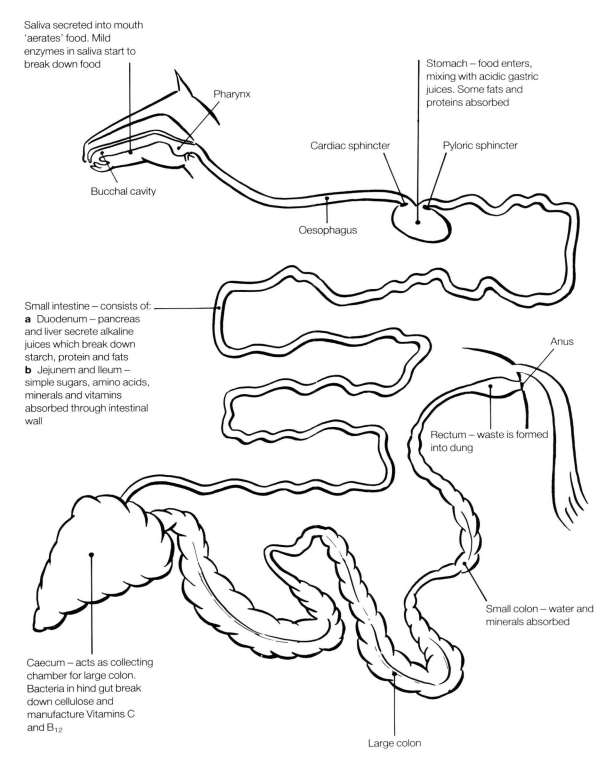

Saliva secreted into mouth 'aerates' food. Mild enzymes in saliva start to break down food

Pharynx

Stomach – food enters, mixing with acidic gastric juices. Some fats and proteins absorbed

Cardiac sphincter

Pyloric sphincter

Bucchal cavity

Oesophagus

Small intestine – consists of:
a Duodenum – pancreas and liver secrete alkaline juices which break down starch, protein and fats
b Jejunem and Ileum – simple sugars, amino acids, minerals and vitamins absorbed through intestinal wall

Anus

Rectum – waste is formed into dung

Small colon – water and minerals absorbed

Caecum – acts as collecting chamber for large colon. Bacteria in hind gut break down cellulose and manufacture Vitamins C and B_{12}

Large colon

Fig. 24 The breakdown of nutrients in the digestive system. Food passes through the digestive system by muscular action called peristalsis

as muscle, but normally the body uses only what it needs and passes the rest out as waste. The normal requirement is 10 per cent of the total feed. This can be increased slightly if the horse is under physical stress, pregnant, growing, lactating or ill (this will be under veterinary supervision). The adult horse does not require higher amounts of protein, as protein has only a 'repair and maintain' role in the fully developed body. However, horses competing in endurance competition may require additional protein, possibly as much as 14 per cent.

High protein concentrate feedstuffs include soya-bean meal (44 per cent), linseed meal (40 per cent) and dried peas (26 per cent). These should be fed in very small amounts, to boost protein levels.

Moderate protein concentrate feedstuffs include oats (10 per cent), and barley (11 per cent). These can make up a large amount of the concentrate ration.

Carbohydrates These are sugars, which provide energy for body functions and movement. They can be found in simple forms such as glucose and starch, which are easy for the body to utilize, or complex forms such as cellulose, which needs to be broken down by the body into simple sugars.

High carbohydrate feedstuffs include peas, beans, soya meal, and maize. These are fed in small amounts when the horse is in strenuous work.

Moderate carbohydrate feedstuffs include barley (moderately high), and oats. These can make up a large amount of the concentrate ration.

Fats and oils (Lipids) Neutral fats are composed of triglyceride molecules, each containing one molecule of Glycerol and three fatty acids. Glycerol can be converted by complex metabolic pathways into glucose and along with the fatty acids can be converted into energy. Fats contain two-and-a-half times more energy than carbohydrates and because of this they are used for endurance horses, especially long distance horses. They normally form only a small part of the diet. Oils play a part in keeping the skin and coat in good condition.

High fat feedstuffs include linseed oil, milk pellets, cod liver oil and vegetable oil.

Low fat feedstuffs include oats, barley, and maize.

Vitamins These are used for growth, repair, digestion and general well-being. They can be divided into two groups:

Fat soluble These are stored in the body, and found in abundance in green foods. They include Vitamins A, D, E and K.

Water Soluble Some of these are synthesized by the micro-organisms found in the horse's gut. They are involved with the metabolism and utilization of the horse's diet. They include: Vitamins B_{1-6}, B_{12}, B-Complex and C.

Minerals Every body process depends on the presence of minerals. When dissolved in body fluids, some minerals can ionize and carry a positive or a negative electrical charge. These substances are called electrolytes and are essential for the normal function of the cells, especially for healthy function of the nerves and muscles. Minerals that are required in large amounts are called macrominerals. These include calcium, phosphorous, magnesium, potassium, sodium and chlorine.

Some minerals are required only in small amounts, but are still essential. The latter group are called microminerals, and include sulphur, iron, copper, zinc, manganese, iodine, selenium, and cobalt.

Water Water makes up about 50–60 per cent of the horse's body weight, so deficiency will cause illness. Water is found in the body cells and the space around the body cells and it is a major constituent of blood. If the horse does not have access to fresh, clean water, dehydration will result, particularly in hot weather. A horse will drink up to 36l (8 gal) of water a day and manufacture a similar amount of saliva. During one hour of moderate work a horse can lose just over 5l (1 gal) of sweat. Excessive fluid loss will cause a mineral imbalance and changes in blood density. This will affect the horse's performance and could result in disease. Water quenches the horse's thirst, helps regulate his body temperature and aids digestion by being a major constituent of bile, saliva and the digestive juices and acting as a transport medium through the gut wall.

Water also aids excretion via the kidneys and by being the basis of sweat. It also has nutritional qualities, containing the minerals calcium, sodium and (in some cases) chlorine.

Rules of feeding

Before formulating a ration for your horse, consider these points:

- Feed little and often. This mimics the horse's natural lifestyle and suits his digestive tract.
- Feed plenty of fibre. This follows the horse's natural feeding habits and helps keep the gut healthy.
- Make changes in feed gradually. The 'gut flora' that live in the horse's caecum and large colon are very sensitive to change, and can be destroyed by sudden changes in diet.
- Feed according to the horse's age. Young horses will require higher protein levels than more mature horses.

- Feed according to the amount of work done. The horse's energy usage will govern the amount of carbohydrate that is required. Overfeeding the stabled horse can result in serious imbalances.
- Feed at regular times each day. A strict routine will make the horse feel mentally more settled, and lessen the risk of colic.
- Feed only good quality foods. This will ensure the horse gains maximum nutritional value from his food. Mould can contain toxins that are bad for the horse.
- Allow at least an hour after feeding before working the horse. This is necessary because of the close proximity of the horse's stomach and diaphragm; a full stomach may interfere with his breathing.
- Keep all mangers and feeding utensils clean to deter rodents and germs.
- Always have fresh water available. It is natural for the horse to drink small amounts whilst he eats.

Total daily intake The horse should eat 2.5 per cent of his total body weight in food, per day. This should be divided between bulk/fibre and concentrated feeds, depending on the work he is doing (**fig. 25**).

Compound feeds

These are formulated rations of feed that provide a balanced diet when fed with hay. They come in a cube form, or as a mix, while in the United States they come in two forms: pellet and sweet feed. They are made up from the normal grain feeds, compounded together, with vitamins and minerals added. There are different levels of compound feed for different types of work, e.g., Pony Cubes, Event Cubes, etc. In the 'high performance' feeds, the car-

Fig. 25 Concentrate to bulk feed ratios

Pie chart of total daily intake

a Horse in light work

b Horse in general work such as training BHS students, hunting

c Horse in high performance work such as 3 day eventing, racing

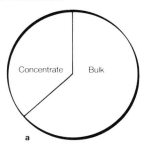

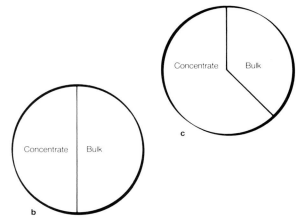

bohydrate and protein content is higher; this is usually achieved by a greater proportion of oats and barley in the mix. The advantages of compound feeds are that they are balanced, the foodstuffs tested for quality, and the bags are easy to store. However, many people make the mistake of mixing, or adding to compound feeds, thus unbalancing them.

Heat-treated feed

Heat-treating some cereal feeds makes the starch more easily digestible. Traditional methods involve boiling the grain in water. This is a good way of swelling the starch, but means that the other nutrients are boiled away. Modern heat treatments include:

Micronizing The grain is passed under an infra-red grill, causing the water content in the grain to vaporize. This breaks down the starch.

Extrusion This method has been used for several years to produce other animal feeds. The cereals are 'pressure cooked' at high temperatures. This causes the starch to swell and crystallize, and can increase the food's digestibility by up to 25 per cent.

Hay

This important constituent of the diet is often fed incorrectly. Fibre is a very important part of the horse's diet: it helps the digestion and break-down of concentrates, and gives the horse a feeling of well-being. It should be fed in small amounts, often, to gain the maximum benefit. Feeding a small amount in the morning and a large amount at night means that some of the concentrate feed will pass into the intestine too quickly, and be only partially digested.

Hay for horses must be of good quality, and contain a high proportion of those grasses with a high digestible value, namely: perennial rye, timothy and cocksfoot (20).

Alfa alfa hay This is fed in the USA, where the climate makes it easier to grow than in the UK. It is a good source of energy and protein, and should be mixed with meadow hay to form the fibre ration.

Haylage/horsehage This is initially made in the same way as hay, but the grass is baled in airtight packs when it is half-dry. This means that it is free from spores and dust. It is expensive, but excellent for horses with respiratory problems when it is fed instead of hay.

Silage This is not commonly fed to horses, as the tendency for it to become acidic when fermenting can lead to botulism (a serious form of food poisoning). If silage is fed, clamp silage is safer than big bale silage.

Hydroponic grass This is barley grass, grown in a machine that creates a controlled environment. It is fed as part of the concentrate ration; it is not a hay substitute. It can be usefully fed to horses in training or at stud, as it is high in protein.

SUMMARY

- Your feed programme must simulate the horse's natural feeding pattern.
- Ensure that your horse's diet contains the correct balance of nutrients.
- Feed each horse as an individual.

20 Rye, timothy and cocksfoot grasses

8
EXERCISE

8
EXERCISE

To maintain health, daily exercise is important. It conditions the horse by activating the digestive, respiratory, circulatory, lymphatic and urinary systems. This, in turn, leads to the correct development of healthy muscles, bones, tendons and other body tissues. In the wild, the horse will browse and wander, eating a diet to maintain himself in a healthy condition. He will not exert himself unless he is fleeing from danger, but he does not suffer the psychological effects of confinement. Confinement can have a poor effect on the horse's mental health. Some horses will develop vices, and become difficult to handle, whereas others will accept their lot, and become dull and dejected.

The Circulatory System

When we stable a horse, we restrict his movement. He will not die from this, but his general health and well-being will be affected. The horse needs to be exercised daily to work off his high spirits and, more importantly, to stimulate his circulation. All his bodily systems work closely together, one reacting to another. The circulatory system and the lymphatic system are the main 'transporters' of nutrients, oxygen and waste, and are therefore essential to the basic life process.

The resting pulse of the horse is 30–40 beats per minute. When moving off into walk the heart rate doubles, and it can go as high as 200 beats per minute when the horse is moving at speed. Controlled, regular exercise will strengthen the muscular heart and gradually develop the circulatory system's ability to transport oxygen and collect waste by increasing the number of blood capillaries in the muscles and lungs (capilliarization). If you work the horse too hard, too soon, then the under-developed circulatory system will be unable to supply enough oxygen to the tissue cells, and will waste away. This will result in fatigue.

Blood, and fluids derived from it, circulate around the body within blood vessels, pumped by the heart. Blood carries oxygen and nutrients to the tissues, carbon dioxide to the lungs and waste to the kidneys. It also controls body temperature, carries hormones to the major organs, and some of its constituents are involved in the defence of injury and infection.

Blood

Blood consists of cells bathed in a fluid called plasma.

Plasma This is a straw-coloured fluid, made up of 92 per cent water, 6 per cent proteins and some mineral salts, with hormones and metabolic waste products making up the other 2 per cent. There are two major types of plasma proteins.

Globulins These develop immunity and fight disease. They make antibodies and fibrinogen, an essential part of blood clotting.

Albumin This is manufactured in the liver. It binds substances together in the blood and because it does not pass readily through the vessel walls, it is responsible for keeping a high osmotic pressure within the circulatory system. This keeps the fluid of the plasma in the blood vessels, and thus maintains an even body fluid balance.

Serum This is plasma without the plasma proteins, which are used in the clotting process of blood.

Blood cells

Red cells (erythrocytes) These cells are coloured red by the pigment haemoglobin. Haemoglobin carries oxygen (as oxyhaemoglobin) from the lungs, and carbon dioxide from the body tissues. Red cells are manufactured in the bone marrow and have a lifespan of about four months, eventually being broken down in the liver, from where iron alone is salvaged.

White cells (leucocytes) There are two main categories of white cells.

a Granulocytes. These are formed in the bone marrow, and include eosinophils, which break down toxins; basophils, which prevent the blood clotting during inflammation; and neutrophils, which fight infection by killing bacteria (forming pus in the process).
b Agranulocytes. These are formed in the lymphatic system and include monocytes, which destroy bacteria, and lymphocytes, which form antibodies, and develop immunity.

Packed cell volume (PCV) This is the term used to describe the number of blood cells per cu. mm of blood, measured in a blood count. During exercise the number of red cells increases, being pushed out of their storage in the spleen. As a horse becomes fitter, his PCV will increase as he will have manufactured more red cells to enable him to carry more oxygen around the body.

Platelets These originate in the bone marrow. They reduce blood loss in the event of injury by sticking to each other, and to the vessel walls to form a plug.

The heart

This is a muscular organ, surrounded by a sack called the pericardium. It is divided into a left and a right side by the septum. Each side has an upper, collecting chamber (atrium), and lower, pumping chamber (ventricle). The heart pumps blood into two circulatory systems: the systemic (around the body), and the pulmonary (through the lungs).

Systemic circulation

This describes the circulation of blood around the body and back to the heart (**fig. 26**). The blood carries oxygenated blood out to the body, via the aorta, into arteries. These divide into arterioles, which ultimately become capillaries, and have close proximity to tissue cells, the blood dropping off the oxygen and picking up carbon dioxide and other waste products. The capillaries then unite to form venules, which unite to form veins and flow back to the main vena cava vein, leading into the heart. Unlike arteries, veins have valves, which ensure that the

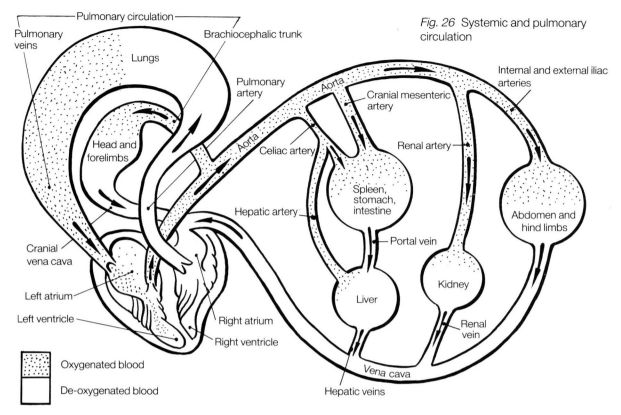

Fig. 26 Systemic and pulmonary circulation

Pulmonary circulation
Pulmonary veins
Lungs
Brachiocephalic trunk
Pulmonary artery
Aorta
Aorta
Head and forelimbs
Celiac artery
Cranial mesenteric artery
Renal artery
Internal and external iliac arteries
Hepatic artery
Spleen, stomach, intestine
Portal vein
Abdomen and hind limbs
Cranial vena cava
Left atrium
Left ventricle
Right atrium
Right ventricle
Liver
Kidney
Renal vein
Oxygenated blood
De-oxygenated blood
Vena cava
Hepatic veins

de-oxygenated blood flows to the heart. The systemic circulation also carries nutrients in the blood from the digestive system, filters the blood through the liver, and takes it back to the heart. From the heart, it is pumped out to the body with the oxygenated blood, through the arteries.

Pulmonary circulations

De-oxygenated blood (bluish in colour) is pumped from the right side of heart, through the pulmonary artery, into the lungs, where the pulmonary artery divides into arterioles, and then capillaries (**fig. 26**). These capillaries run through the alveoli (air sacs), dropping off carbon dioxide, and picking up oxygen. The returning capillaries unite to form venules, and these unite to run into the pulmonary vein, that carries the oxygenated blood (now bright red in colour) back

to the heart. This is the only instance where an artery carries de-oxygenated blood, and a vein carries oxygenated blood.

The lymphatic system

This system works closely with the circulatory system, and consists of a network of vessels carrying lymph. Like veins, the system requires the contraction of muscles to push the lymph along the vessels so is most effective when the horse is being exercised.

Lymph This is a clear, colourless liquid, similar to plasma. It is derived from excess tissue fluid that has not been absorbed by the venules. It carries lymphocytes, glucose, proteins and waste products. It filters out noxious substances and absorbs them, thus fighting infection. Sometimes, if the protein balance in the

lymph has been upset, it will seep through the vessel walls, and accumulate in the body tissues (oedema). This is particularly noticeable in the legs.

Lymph vessels These are similar to veins, having valves that ensure that the lymph flows only *towards* the heart. They start as lymph capillaries in the tissue cells and unite to form vessels. They flow through lymph glands, that filter the lymph and destroy any infection. The lymph vessels enter the blood stream at the vena cava.

The Effects of Exercise on Muscles, Bones and Tendons

Muscles

Exercise affects mainly the voluntary, striated, skeletal muscle. The other types of muscle are the smooth, involuntary muscle of the digestive, circulatory, respiratory and urogenital systems, and the striated, involuntary cardiac muscle of the heart.

Skeletal muscle This consists of a bundle of fibres, each fibre containing a muscle cell (**fig. 27**). These fibres are joined together by a membrane called the sarcolemma. The sarcolemma also connects the muscle to the tendon. Exercise does not develop more muscles, but causes the fibres of the existing muscles to increase in size (hypertrophy), and increases the vascular supply to the muscles (capilliarization). This increases the blood's efficiency in transporting oxygen to the muscle, and carrying waste (lactic acid) away. The best muscle performance is gained from the muscles working with oxygen (aerobically). Muscles can function without oxygen (anaerobically) for short periods; how-

ever, over a long period of anaerobic activity they will fatigue, and create excessive amounts of lactic acid, which will damage the muscle fibres. All work done will help develop muscle. However, encouraging the horse to work in a correct and balanced way in all gaits will ensure correct muscle development and improved performance.

Bone

This is made up of the protein collagen, on which calcium phosphate is deposited. Collagen gives bone its viability whilst the calcium phosphate gives it its density. The bone is surrounded by a membrane called the periosteum, which connects it to tendons and ligaments. Within this membrane are cells called osteoblasts, which continously form new bone (ossification), while old bone is destroyed by cells called osteoclasts. Controlled exer-

Fig. 27 Muscle fibre

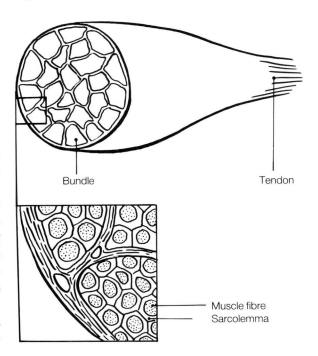

Bundle

Tendon

Muscle fibre
Sarcolemma

cise affects the bone by causing it to change shape in response to the work in those areas that are stressed, and to replenish the deposits of calcium phospate, thus improving the bone's density. Road exercise will improve the density of the bone, most benefit being gained by walking the horse with only short bursts of trot. Excessive trotting on the roads will have a concussive effect, which could be harmful in the long term.

Tendons

These connect muscle to bone. The long tendons of the lower limbs are particularly susceptible to damage. Tendons are made up of the protein collagen which forms long strands of fibres that are formed from cells called fibroblasts. In nature, new collogen is layed down about every six to 12 months. Controlled exercise will cause a faster replenishment of the collagen, thus strengthening the tendons. This is best done by walking on the roads, particularly in the early part of the fitness programme.

Controlled Exercise

Under saddle

For the horse to gain benefit from exercise, we must exert some stress on his body. This has to be controlled, however, as overstress will cause damage and fatigue. A tired horse is far more likely to damage himself, as his movements will lose some co-ordination. Experience shows that excessive hard work on hard surfaces will overstress and damage the bone.

Stamina is something that is 'built into' the horse, to a certain extent, but can be developed by asking the horse to exert himself over different terrain. It is difficult to get the right balance between stress and overstress, but you should be able to recognize when your horse is fatigued, and you should not push him too much. If he is tired, you should ask him to perform the same work at a slower speed for a while, and then ask for more on another day.

The first six to eight weeks of any fitness programme should be spent working the horse steadily on the roads. Avoid excessive trotting work on the roads, particularly in the early stages as this will cause damaging concussion to the horse's legs.

Lungeing

This can be a useful form of exercise and training. However, remember that work on a circle is very stressful on the horse's joints, so 20 to 30 minutes is sufficient to exercise the horse without straining it unduly. It is important to vary the work on the lunge so that the horse uses all his muscles equally. This can be done by changing the rein at least every three to four minutes and by using transitions to improve the horse's balance. For safety, the handler should wear gloves to protect his hands in case the horse becomes strong. A hard hat is also advisable, particularly if the horse is high-spirited, as he may well kick out his heels.

It is best to have an enclosed area for lungeing with a level surface that provides good footing. This will enable you to lunge confidently and the horse will be more attentive and work correctly. Grassland can tend to be either too slippery or too hard, so it may be worth considering an all-weather surface, although this will be expensive.

Lunge equipment should provide con-

trol, encourage the horse to work correctly and give protection where necessary. The lunge cavesson and lunge rein will provide control; especially when used with a bridle and side reins, as these will encourage the horse to work in a more correct and balanced way. The side reins attach to the bit and will need to be secured to either a saddle or a lunge roller. They should be short enough to encourage the horse to work shorter and rounder, but not so short that the horse pulls or leans on them. With skilful lungeing it is possible to improve the horse's suppleness, but often the horse may knock himself, particularly around the fetlock area. It is best, therefore, to avoid the risk of injury by attaching brushing boots.

Ride and lead

This can be useful if your horses are good on the roads, and you have a number to exercise. You should not attempt to ride and lead on the roads until you have practised in a field at home. Some horses will refuse to work together, others will become too excited. The lead horse must wear a bridle for control and be led either with the reins or a lead rope and coupling chain attached to the bit. Knee boots are also advisable, particularly for the lead horse, as he does not have the rider to balance him.

Keep the lead horse on the side away from the traffic, keep his head in line with your knee but still allow him enough rein to use his neck to balance. If the lead horse gets in front of your knee, he will tend to race the ridden horse; behind your knee, he may well get kicked. An important part of the fitness programme is to carry the weight of the rider. Therefore, if possible you should alternate between riding and leading the horses from day to day.

Care of the Horse after Exercise

Regular, controlled exercise promotes good health and condition. Once the circulation has been stimulated, the body temperature will rise, and the horse will cool himself by sweating. However, great care must be taken after exercise to ensure that the horse is comfortable and cooled down correctly. The following must be taken into consideration:

Pulse and respiration The horse should be walked for the last half mile home so that the heart rate and respiration can drop. If the horse is left standing in the stable blowing, with a high heart rate, he will suffer distress. If he is rugged his body temperature will rise due to the blood circulating quickly and bringing heat to the skin surface. It will then fall quickly, which could cause a chill.

Removing tack It is important after dismounting, particularly if you have been riding for any length of time, to loosen the girth and leave the saddle on the horse for five or ten minutes, to allow blood to flow slowly back into the area under the saddle. Then gently rub the area to aid circulation.

Grooming and clothing If the horse has been walked until his respiration has dropped he will have probably stopped sweating and started to dry off. However, the heart rate at walk is still twice as high as the resting pulse, so his circulation will still be stimulated and his body temperature raised. When standing in the stable, his heart rate will fall, and his body temperature drop fairly quickly, so care must be taken to prevent him catching a chill.

In hot weather, washing the horse with warm water after exercise, drying him off

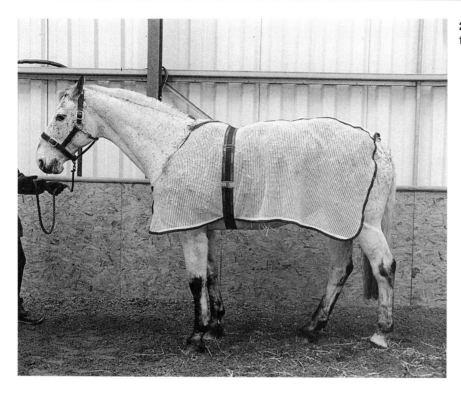

21 A horse correctly thatched

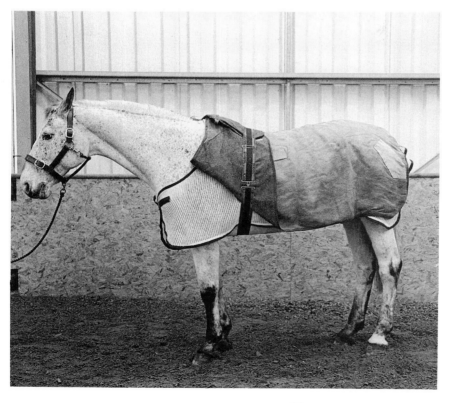

22 A sweat sheet and jute rug correctly fitted to a horse after exercise

thoroughly and then walking in hand for five or ten minutes will ensure that he returns to his stable dry and clean. This will also reduce the amount of grooming needed. Unless the weather is very hot, you may need to put on a cotton summer sheet or cooler rug.

In cold weather some people will still wash down their horses, but this is really only advisable if you have a solarium or heat lamps to dry off your horse. The best way of cooling a horse off is to groom him thoroughly (strapping – see Chapter 9). This stimulates the circulation, so slows the cooling process. It is important that the horse is kept partially covered with a rug, particularly over his loins. If you are unable to groom him straight away, then you must rug him. The choice of rugs is important: over-rugging, whilst the horse is still warm will cause his body temperature to rise quickly and then fall quickly when he starts to sweat, leaving him shivering in damp rugs. There are various alternative methods of cooling your horse after exercise.

Thatching   Straw is placed under a jute rug or sweat sheet (**21**). The legs may also be thatched by putting straw under stable bandages. The aim is to trap air between the body and the rug. This air then warms as the body temperature drops. This method is rarely used today, as fewer horses are bedded on straw, and some modern rug fabrics have made it unnecessary.

Sweat sheets   A sweat sheet is placed under another rug, and works on the same principle as thatching (**22**). The front of the top rug may be folded back. If so, take care that the breast buckle is in front of the roller, to prevent undue pressure on the back. It is important that the top rug is made of a 'breathable' fabric such as wool, cotton or jute. Many modern nylon stable rugs are not suitable. After about 20 minutes both rugs should be replaced with the horse's normal, dry rugs.

Cooler sheets   These are made of modern fabrics with thermal qualities. They allow the moisture out and air in, yet remain dry against the body. After about 20 minutes, this should be changed, and the horse's normal, dry rugs put on.

Bandaging   Some people will stable bandage directly after exercise, particularly if the exercise has been strenuous. Although there is no scientific evidence to support it, it does help to prevent, 'filled legs', and this could be because keeping the area warm stimulates the circulation.

SUMMARY

- The stabled horse must be exercised to stimulate his respiratory and cardiovascular systems.
- Controlled exercise will improve the horse's health.
- It is important to get the right balance between stress and overstress when exercising.
- Correct care of the horse must be taken after exercise.

9
PRESENTATION OF THE HORSE

9
PRESENTATION OF THE HORSE

The skin and coat reflect the health of the horse. Horses in good condition have a supple skin and a shine to the coat, even if they are living out. We groom, clip and wash the horse to improve his appearance, but we must remember that our main priority is the health and condition of the horse, and these tasks play important roles in this area.

The Skin and Coat

The skin plays an important role in the horse's defence system (fig. 28). It acts as barrier to germs, a sophisticated body temperature control, and its sensitivity to touch, heat and pain is vital to the horse's well-being, and even his survival.

The skin has two layers. The outer layer (the epidermis) is made up of several layers of soft tissue; the outermost of which is made of the protein keratin which, along with the hair, forms a lifeless protective barrier. The bottom layer of the epidermis produces new cells, which gradually work their way to the surface, finally being shed as dandruff. The thicker, inner layer is the dermis. This lies on top of a layer of subcutaneous fat, to which it is loosely attached, thus giving skin its mobility. The dermis contains the sweat glands, blood and lymph vessels and nerve endings. Under the subcutaneous layer of fat is a sheet of muscle called the panniculus muscle. This enables the horse to 'twitch' his skin and dislodge flies etc. The skin of fine quality horses, such as thoroughbreds, is thinner than that of native breeds.

Sweating

This is part of the horse's temperature control mechanism, and is also a method of excreting waste products. Sweating cools the horse by taking away latent heat during evaporation. All over the body there are sweat glands, which excrete onto the outer layer of the skin.

The Reasons for Grooming

The skin of the stabled horse should be groomed to spread the oil secreted by the sebaceous glands (fig. 29) This gives the skin and coat its elasticity and shine. It will also remove dead skin, which in the wild would be removed naturally by mud and sweat, and by the horse rolling. Grooming also improves skin hygiene, and therefore helps to prevent disease. Circulation is an important factor to be considered, as the stabled horse is unable to move freely and keep himself warm. By

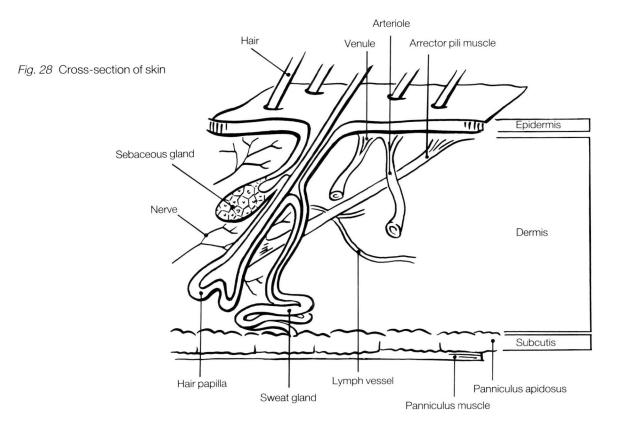

Fig. 28 Cross-section of skin

grooming thoroughly we stimulate the circulation, which promotes the health of the skin, and is also important when drying off a hot horse after exercise. When a horse is in training the skin will become stronger, as the increase in circulation to the skin will stimulate an increase in production of skin cells, and therefore an increase in dead cells that must be brushed away.

Quartering

This is the term used for the quick preparation of the horse in the morning before exercise. It is also a good time to check the horse for any injury he may have sustained during the night. Some people say that the term 'quartering' is used because if the horse is rugged, you should never remove all its rugs, but fold them in quarters as you groom. Others say that it derives from the days when horses were kept in stalls; you first groomed all the hindquarters, and then turned the horses round and groomed their fronts. If the horse is rugged, the rugs should be removed and straightened after quartering.

Quartering procedure
- Tie up the horse.
- Pick out his feet into a skip (you do not want him to tread in the muck again). You should pay particular attention to the state of his shoeing, and check that the frog is healthy. If there is an offensive smell, and the frog seems shrivelled and soft, he is suffering from thrush.
- Quickly go over the horse with a body brush or stable rubber. Remove any

Fig. 29 The grooming kit

a Body brush – made of short soft bristles to remove scurf from skin

b Dandy brush – made of hard natural bristles. Used to remove mud, but not around delicate areas such as the head

c Metal curry comb – used to clean brushes, but not horse

d Rubber curry comb – used to loosen scurf before grooming

e Hoof pick with brush – allows you to pick and brush away muck thoroughly

f Massage pad – has replaced hay wisp in toning muscles

g Two sponges – one for eyes and nose, one for dock

h Stable rubber – used to remove excess dust after grooming

stable stains with a water brush and some warm water.

- Brush out the mane and tail. You may wish to apply a tail bandage if the tail is pulled.
- Sponge out the eyes, nose and dock (**23**). Remember to untie the horse when handling his head. Also, you must not use the same sponge for the eyes that you have used for the dock, as the anus is a site for bacteria. Always sponge the eyes downwards, taking the debris away from the eye.
- If the horse is rugged, brush off any bedding or muck on the rug.

Strapping

This is the term used for the thorough grooming of the horse. The term is derived from when people that groomed horses were called 'strappers'. It is best done straight after exercise, as the circulation will have toned the skin and the grooming will help to keep the horse warm as his circulation drops after work,

and thus prevent him catching a chill. You should also check for any injury that may have occurred during exercise.

Strapping procedure

- Tie up the horse.
- You may have already washed the feet, but they must also be picked out and the state of the foot checked.
- Unless you are grooming a sensitive-skinned thoroughbred, it is a good idea to first loosen the dandruff with a rubber curry comb. Gently go over the body, working in circular motions.
- Thoroughly brush the horse with the body brush, keeping it clean by regularly scraping it with a metal curry comb. If you groom as much as possible with the hand nearest to the horse (the left hand on his near side, and the right hand on his off side), you can use your body-weight behind the brush (**24**). Brush in a circular, 'flicking' motion to remove the dirt.

(Opposite) **23** Gently sponge the eye downwards

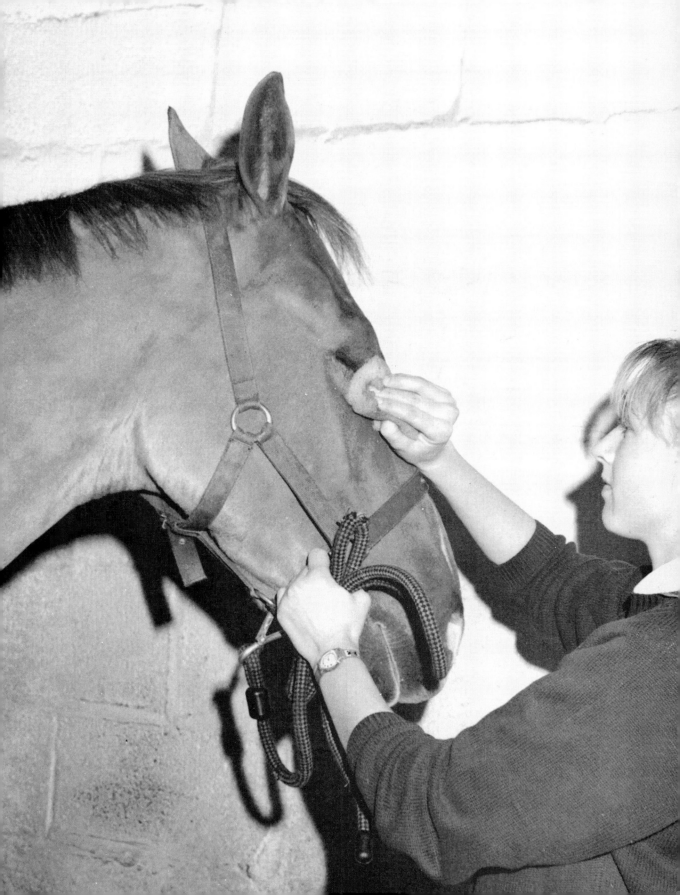

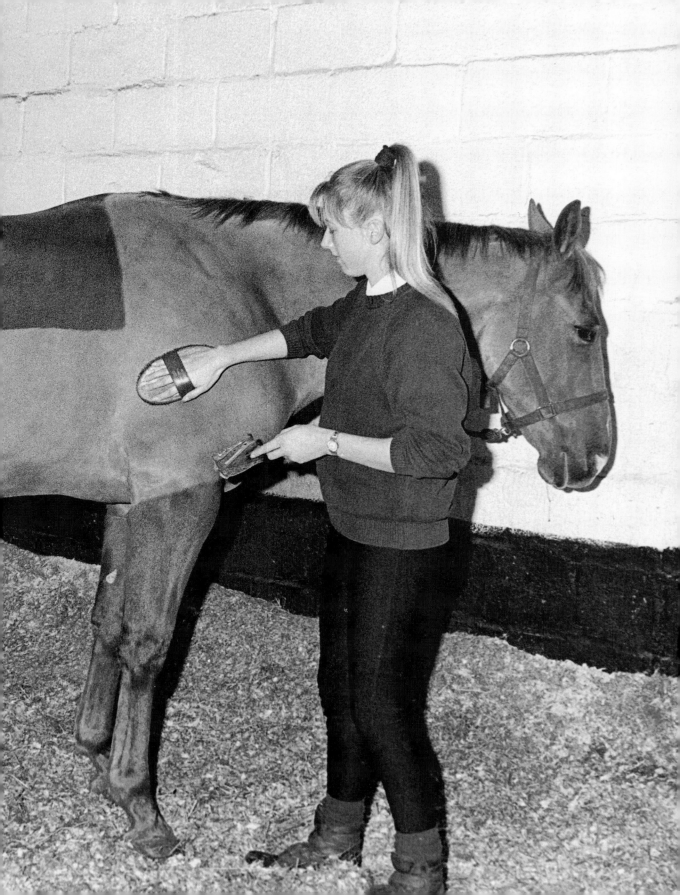

- Thoroughly brush out the mane and tail with the body brush, carefully brushing the dandruff out from the roots.
- Rub the horse over with a stable rubber. This removes the grease that has been brought to the surface.
- Gently sponge the eyes, nose and dock.
- Clean the sheath or teats as appropriate. This is best done with a mild soap and warm water.
- If the horse is rugged, the rugs should be removed, shaken clean and replaced.
- Damp down the mane and tail with a water brush and apply a tail bandage if desired.

Wisping

This may be done as part of the strapping. It is the term used to describe the method of toning and massaging the main superficial muscles. Traditionally it was done with a dampened hay wisp, but today specially shaped pads are often used. Take care not to wisp where the bones are prominent, as this will cause bruising (**fig. 30**).

Washing

There are many 'coat care' products on the market today. They all claim to make the coat healthier and shinier. This is, of course, impossible. A healthy coat comes from a healthy diet and good management. Washing the coat too often with soap will make it dry, as it washes away the natural oils. Conditioners do not have the same effect as the sebum oil naturally secreted by the horse. It is very difficult to plait a mane or tail that has just been washed as the hair is slippery and the thread tends not to hold. However, during the summer, hosing down the horse after work, without using soap, can be very refreshing for him, and helps to keep his coat and skin healthy. In some yards, solariums are built so that the horses can be washed all year round and placed under them in cold weather to dry. Sometimes it may be necessary to wash the horse with medical shampoo to alleviate problem skin conditions.

Washing procedure
- It is better to wash the horse with lukewarm to hand-hot water, even in

Fig. 30 Areas of muscles to wisp

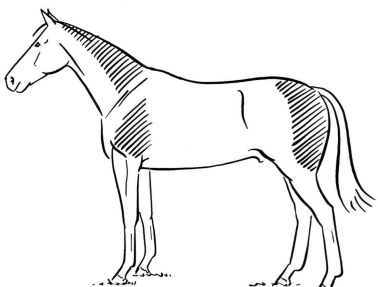

(Opposite) **24** Groom using the hand nearest the horse's body

hot weather. Horses, quite naturally, object to cold water.

- If shampoo is used, it must be thoroughly rinsed out after washing. Use non-perfumed, mild shampoo, as this is less likely to cause irritation.
- Be sure to dry the horse off thoroughly afterwards. It may be necessary to walk him in hand for a while. If a sweat scraper is used, be careful not to damage risen surface blood vessels.

Clipping

The horse grows his coat in the winter months to keep warm. It is shed again in the spring when the warmer weather arrives. During the winter, you will probably need to clip your horse if he is working. This keeps him in better condition, and makes it easier to keep him clean. A sweaty horse dries from his skin to the tips of his hair; thus a horse with a long coat will be left with a damp film of cold sweat long after he has cooled down, and this can cause a chill.

Clip when the winter coat has 'set'. In the northern hemisphere, this is at about the end of October. You should repeat the clip as often as necessary. Horses differ, but you can clip the horse until the end of February without damaging his summer coat. If you do clip after that time, the horse will not grow a good summer coat; if you are eventing during the spring or summer, you will probably need to continue clipping anyway. Horses with a thick summer coat will need clipping.

The clipping box

If you have only a small yard, it is not practical to have a box just for clipping. In this case, you should clear out the horse's stable, and put a small amount of bedding down, which can be swept out afterwards,

along with the hair. You should improvise to create the following conditions as much as possible:

- The clipping box should be situated in a quiet part of the yard.
- The box must be well lit, so extra lighting may have to be fitted, even if temporarily.
- The box should be a good size, so that you can move around the horse safely.
- The floor should be covered with rubber matting, so that both you and the horse are earthed.

Fig. 31 Full clip: often given the first few times for hunters or eventers, especially if they tend to be hairy

Fig. 34 Trace clip: so-called because it follows the line of the traces of carriage harness. Useful for field-kept horses, as the neck retains some protection

- The electric socket should be set reasonably high, and there should be a system of hanging the clipping machine's wire above head height. There should be a circuit breaker attached to the electric socket to prevent any electric shocks. Most modern clippers have them built in anyway, but it is as well to take the extra precaution.
- There should be several tie-up rings so that you can move the horse about the box easily, to clip the different areas of the body.

The clippers

There are several types of machine on the market today. Modern machines tend to be quieter and lighter than old-fashioned clippers. You can buy cordless, battery-operated clippers that are useful for clipping the head and trimming the horse's heels, while a larger, more heavy-duty machine is necessary to clip the body.

Even if you only have one horse, you should have at least three sets of blades, so that you can use two sets to clip and

Fig. 32 Hunter clip: protection is left on the legs and saddle area

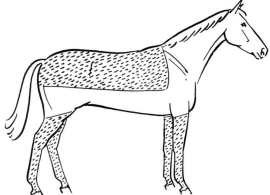

Fig. 33 Blanket clip: a very useful clip for stabled horses, especially if they are likely to be left standing around, as the loins are left covered

Fig. 35 Chaser clip: this leaves hair on the main galloping muscles, thus keeping them warm

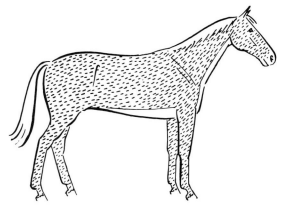

Fig. 36 Neck and belly clip: useful for ponies, or horses in light work

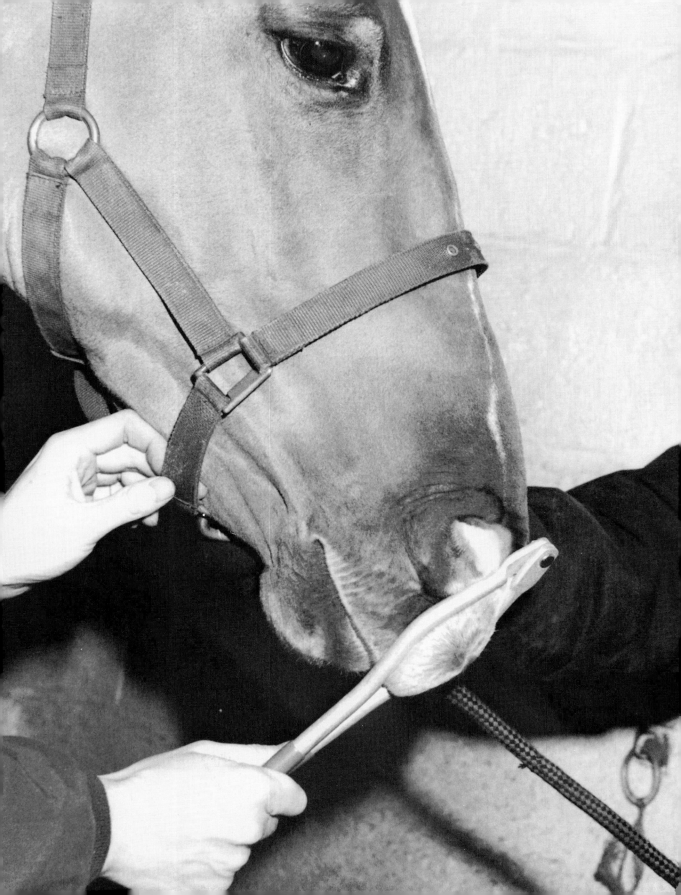

have one set being sharpened. There are different types of blades available.

Fine blades cut very close to the skin. Skill is needed to use these as they do not allow for uneven clipping, and will give a poor finish if incorrectly used. Medium blades are in general use for most clips. Coarse blades are also called leg plates. They are used to clip the legs, as they do not clip too close, so leave some protection.

Care should be taken with the blades, as they break easily if dropped. You must not clip with blunt blades, as they will hurt the horse and damage the clippers.

Clothing

Horse hair can be very irritating for the clipper, particularly when you clip the second or third time as it has become short and bristly. A boiler suit or something similar is practical wear. If you have long hair, tie it back, or you may lose it! Wear rubber-soled boots to help earth you, particularly if you do not clip on rubber matting.

It is a good idea to have an old blanket to cover the horse whilst he is being clipped, to prevent him becoming chilled. The hair can get into the rugs and be very irritating, so keep this blanket just for this purpose.

Clipping procedure

- The horse must be clean and dry. This will mean that the blades will clip more easily, and therefore do a better job.
- It is a good idea to bandage the tail and, if the horse has not been clipped before, plait the mane, so that it does not get caught up in the blades.
- If the horse has not been clipped before you should have an assistant to hold

him. Run the clippers away from the horse to accustom him to the noise, and then run it against the horse's shoulder without actually clipping. Usually it is not the noise of the machine that horses object to, but the vibration of the blades against the skin.

- Clip in long strokes into the coat, keeping an even pressure on the horse. Always clip *against* the lie of the coat, for the best results.
- When the horse seems quiet, he should be given a haynet.
- When clipping the head, you should protect the horse's eyes with one hand, whilst clipping with the other. Ask an assistant to hold the head steady.

Care of the machine

It is important to get the tension of the blades correct. Basically, they should be as loose as possible but still cut easily. If they are too tight, they will heat quickly and strain the machine. Follow the manufacturer's instructions to set the tension right. Whilst you are clipping, you should periodically run the blades through non-acidic oil to lubricate them. Some people run the blades through a mixture of oil and paraffin to cool them. This can cause a skin reaction and does tend to rust the blades.

When you have finished clipping, the blades should be removed and the whole machine thoroughly cleaned, especially the air filters. An oily rag should be folded around the blades. At the end of the season, the clippers should be sent away to be serviced.

Twitching the horse

Horses can be ticklish, especially around the stifles and elbows. If the horse becomes restless, you may have to 'twitch' him to restrain him (**25**). A twitch is applied to the top lip, and it is thought

25 Using a humane twitch

26 Pulling a mane – **a** place the comb in the mane at the desired length

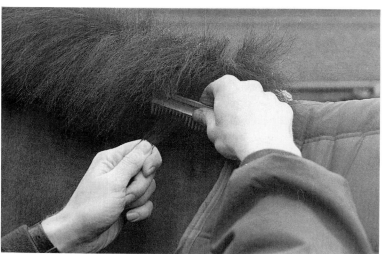

27 Pulling a mane – **b** comb up the mane, and pull with the fingers

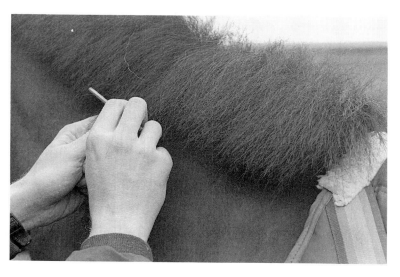

28 Pulling a mane – **c** continue up the neck, gradually

(Opposite) **29** A singeing lamp

that applying pressure to this area causes endorphins to be released into the blood, which have a tranquillizing effect. The practice of twitching the ear is barbaric. If a horse is that nervous, it should be sedated with drugs by your vet. Another form of restraint is to pinch a fold of skin on the neck. This can help to keep the horse still whilst you clip sensitive areas.

Trimming

This is done mainly for appearance. Some breeds have their own 'dress code' for showing, so check before starting.

Mane pulling The mane should be pulled so that it is 3–4in (8–10cm) long, and so that it lies on the right-hand side. You pull the mane using fingers and comb, although care should be taken not to break the hair with the comb, as it will cause the mane to stick up (**26**). If you get sore fingers pulling the mane, then you have pulled out too large a chunk of mane, and your horse will soon start to object to having his mane pulled (**27**). It is easier to pull a mane when the horse has worked, or in warm weather, as the skin pores are open (**28**).

Tail pulling This should be done gradually, over several days. The hairs should be plucked from the side. It can be useful to rub resin on the fingers to pluck the smaller hairs, as it makes the fingers sticky.

Heels These should be trimmed against the lie of the coat to give a smooth finish.

Beard and whiskers These should be clipped to the roots. Do not clip off all the whiskers around the muzzle, as they act as 'feelers' in the dark.

Singeing This is very rarely done today, as it is difficult to buy a singeing lamp (**29**). However, it is a very effective way of tidying up the horse's whiskers and the coarse 'cat hairs' that grow on a clipped horse in the spring.

Plaiting

This is done for appearance, and in some showing classes is considered correct turn-out. Plaiting does give an extra touch of elegance, although not many people tend to bother with sewing the plaits in, which is the traditionally correct

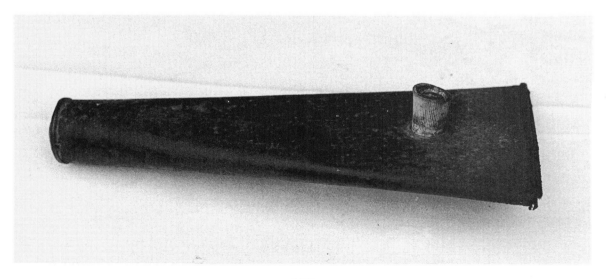

Fig. 37 Plaiting a mane

a Divide mane into sections

b Plait mane tightly and wrap cotton around end of plait

c Stitch plait by passing needle underneath and through to top of plait

d Pass needle through loop of plait and repeat

e Plait stitched to hide cotton

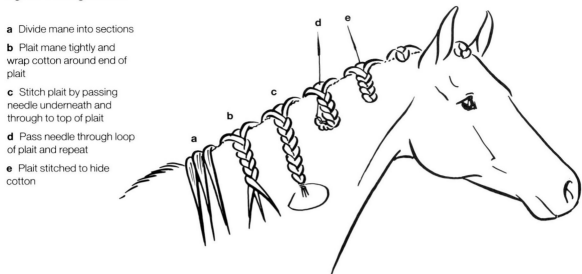

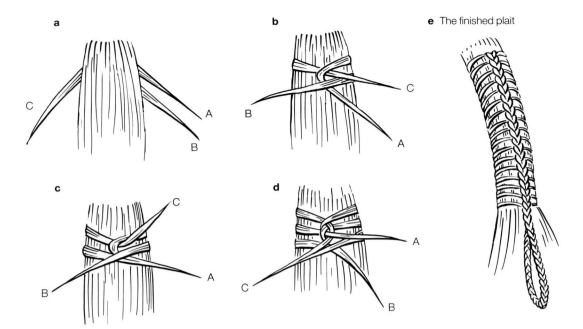

Fig. 38 Plaiting a tail

a Take three sections of hair from underneath the tail; two sections from the right side (A, B) and one from the left side (C)

b Cross section A over section C and start plait

c As you continue down the tail, add more hair from underneath to each section

d Keep the plait tight and continue unitl 2.5cm (1in) before the end of the dock

e Plait the end and stitch in place. With this style of plaiting, the plait will be raised

way, but opt for elastic bands instead. With a correctly sewn mane, you should not see the cotton thread **(fig. 37)**. There is a trend, with dressage horses, to plait small sausage-shaped plaits and wrap white tape around them. The size and type of plait that you use must suit your horse, that is, large hunters do not want small show plaits. Careful plaiting can certainly make a horse look a better shape. Some people will plait their horse the night before a competition, but this can have a detrimental effect on their horse's state of mind and subsequent performance, as he may be agitated at the prospect of competing.

There are two common methods of plaiting the tail, but the traditional way is to plait with the braid raised **(fig. 38)**.

SUMMARY

- The stabled horse must be groomed to promote health.
- Trimming the horse will improve his appearance.
- Clipping will be necessary if the horse is to work at all strenuously.
- Correct and careful plaiting can improve the horse's appearance.

30 A well turned-out horse

10
CLOTHING AND SADDLERY

10
CLOTHING AND SADDLERY

Rugs

The choice of horse clothing available today is very wide ranging. The development of lightweight, warm fabrics has made clothing the stabled horse much easier. The use of thermal cloth gives some rugs a 'breathing' quality, which enables you to use them for keeping horses warm, or for cooling them off. Modern fabrics are also easier to wash and store. Whichever type of clothing you use, you must remember that it should keep the horse warm to maintain condition, and possibly offer some protection from injury.

Whichever type of rug you use, it must fit correctly, particularly around the horse's chest (**fig. 39**). Great care is taken choosing correctly fitting saddlery, which the horse probably wears for a couple of hours a day, but rugs, worn for the remaining 22 hours, are often fitted poorly, if at all. Ill-fitting rugs will slip, will not keep the horse warm, and will rub.

Traditional rugs

Day rug So called because it was originally used during the day, in smart stables, for appearance. Made of fine wool cloth, called melton, it is a fairly warm rug. Today such rugs are usually used for appearance when travelling to competitions.

Jute Jute is a tough material, made from the bark of an East Indian plant. Being very hard-wearing, jute rugs are used as night rugs, or general stable rugs. They should be lined with wool for comfort.

Summer sheet Made of cotton, and used on the stabled horse in summer to keep him clean, and also warm during chilly summer evenings.

Sweat sheets These were actually designed to be put on horses as they are being walked to dry off. The holes allow air to pass down the body. Under another rug, they have the 'string vest' effect of trapping air between the body and the rug, making the horse warmer. They do not serve much purpose used on their own on a sweaty horse stood in the stable.

Blankets Several layers of thin blankets are much warmer than a couple of thick blankets, as air is trapped between the layers, and the horse's body temperature will heat the air (**fig. 40**). A popular traditional type of blanket is the colourful

Fig. 39 Fitting a rug

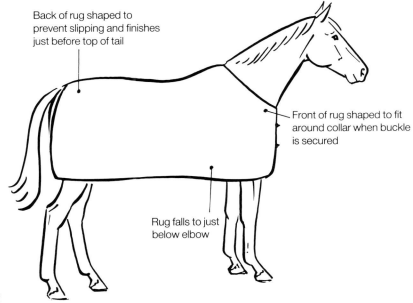

Back of rug shaped to
prevent slipping and finishes
just before top of tail

Front of rug shaped to fit
around collar when buckle
is secured

Rug falls to just
below elbow

Fig. 40 Fitting an under-blanket

a

b

a Place blanket over withers

b Unfold until croup covered

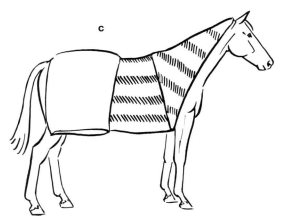

c

c Fold back point of blanket and place folded rug over quarters

d Unfold rug to cover tail end of blanket

woollen 'London blanket'. The purpose of the stripes is to enable you to get the blanket level on the horse, therefore the stripes should run long ways to the horse. However, often the blankets are not made in such a way that makes this possible.

Fillet strings These are essential with traditional rugs to help keep them in place.

Rollers There are a variety available, but all should be used with padding underneath.

Anti-cast rollers There is debate as to how effective these are **(fig. 41)**. However, one problem with them is that they can press into the horse's back when he is lying down.

All these rugs are fitted with a roller or surcingle, and sometimes with a breast girth as well. Modern rugs have dispensed with this, using cross-over surcingles instead, which do not put pressure on the horse's back. However, they must fit, and be adjusted correctly, or they will slip **(31)**.

Modern rugs

Quarter sheet This is made of fine wool, and used to keep a horse with a hunter or full clips warm when being exercised in cold weather **(32)**.

New Zealand rug Again, there are many new fabrics available other than traditional canvas. It is essential that a rugged, stabled horse wears one of these if turned out. These rugs do not necessarily keep him warm, just dry, so it may be necessary to put another rug underneath **(33)**.

Bandages

Care must be taken to fit bandages correctly and, where necessary, to provide enough padding under them for protection. For protection whilst exercising or travelling, bandages have mostly been replaced by boots. However, bandages still play an important role in medical care (see Chapter 5), especially with modern fabrics, some of which have therapeutic qualities.

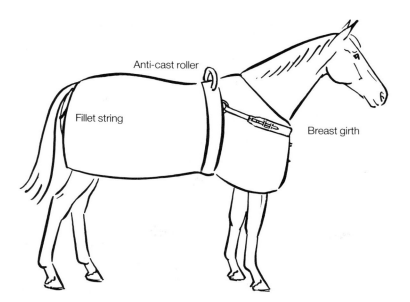

Anti-cast roller

Fillet string

Breast girth

Fig. 41 Fitting an anti-cast roller, breast girth and fillet string

(Top right) **31** A modern, shaped rug

(Bottom right) **32** A quarter sheet

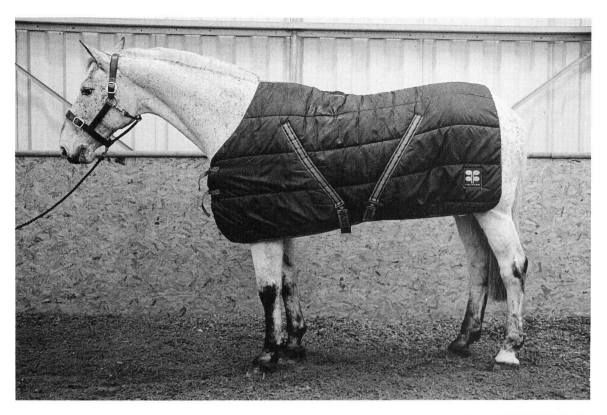

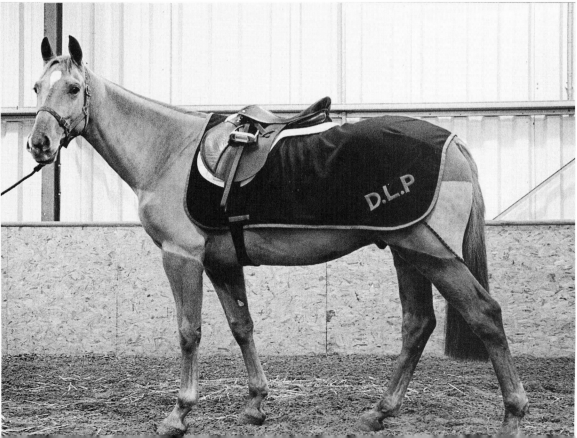

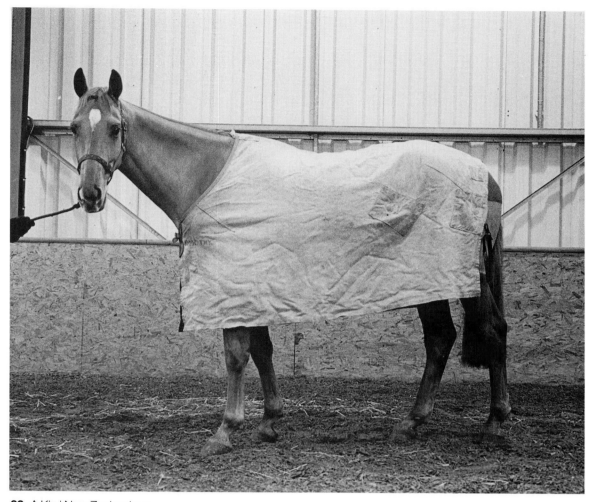

33 A Kiwi New Zealand rug

Stable bandages

These bandages are 2.5m (8ft) long and about 11cm (4½in) wide. They are traditionally made of wool, although there are many different types of fabric used, including thermal cloth. Stable bandages are used to keep the horse warm, particularly if his legs have been clipped. They should be fitted over thin padding to provide extra warmth (**fig. 42**). They are sometimes used to stop legs filling, by encouraging better circulation in the area. Horses that suffer from arthritic conditions in the lower leg certainly work better if kept bandaged in the stable.

Exercise bandages

These are slightly shorter than stable bandages, about 8–10cm (3–4in) wide, and are made of crepe or stockinette (**34**). They are not commonly used now for exercise, as they have been replaced by boots. You should never fit just one exercise bandage: always bandage the opposite leg too, as it will ensure that both legs are used the same way. These bandages are sometimes used to give support if a horse has damaged a tendon, and are still commonly used for protection when going cross-country. To give adequate protection they must cover the sesamoid bones

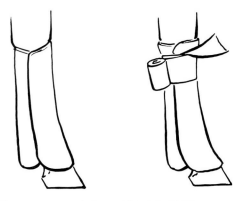

a Place gamgee or similar padding around leg

b,c Wrap bandage around leg in same direction as padding, at a slight downwards angle, keeping an even pressure

d Secure bandage at top with tapes to outside

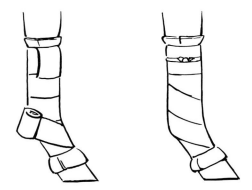

Fig. 42 Applying stable bandages

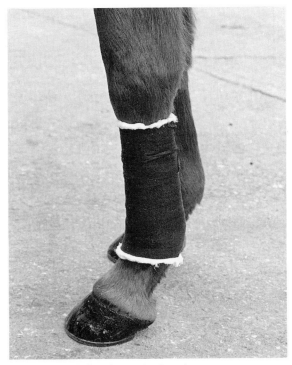

34 A correctly fitted exercise bandage

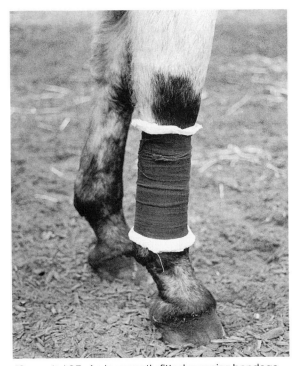

(Opposite) **35** An incorrectly fitted exercise bandage. This offers no support or protection around the fetlock, where it is most needed

at the back of the fetlock, as these are vulnerable, particularly when a horse lands after jumping; the horse's fetlock can hit the ground, causing these bones to shatter (**35**). However, if the bandages are too low, they will interfere with the fetlock-joint movement, and tend to slip. The bandage should be fastened by sewing it to itself. People often use tape, but this can cause pressure and damage to the tendons. When competing, many people now use self-adhesive, disposable bandages. Adequate padding must be used under these bandages, as the self-adhesive quality tends to exert considerable pressure.

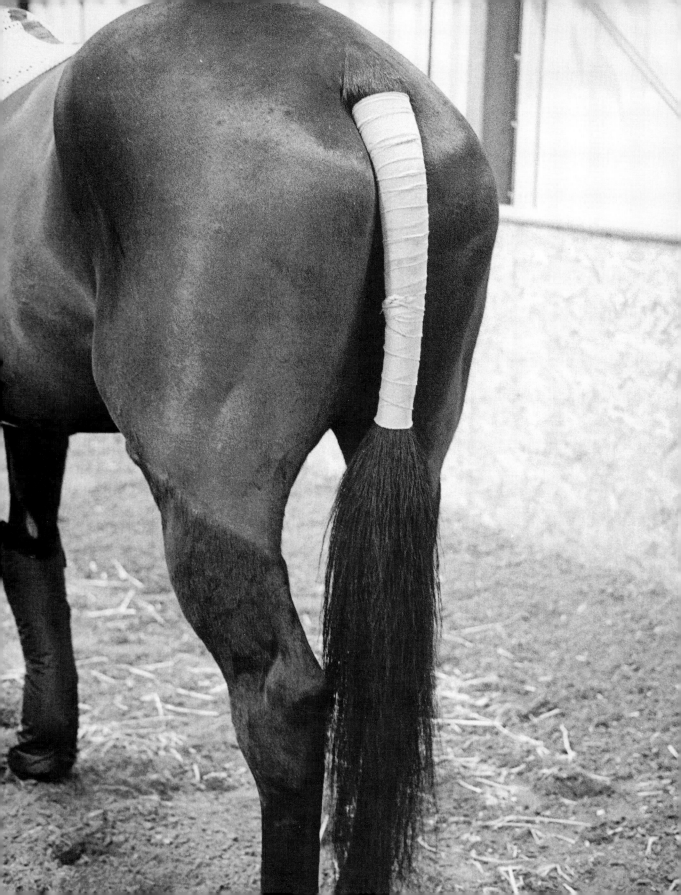

Tail bandages

These are made of elasticated cotton, and are 8cm (3in) wide and 3m (10ft) long. They are used on the stabled horse to improve the appearance of a pulled tail. They should never be fitted too tightly, or left on for too long, as they can restrict the circulation in the dock (**36**).

Saddlery

Choosing the correct saddlery for your horse requires an appreciation of his physical structure, and some knowledge about the effect of different types of equipment on the horse's way of going. The choice in design and style is extensive. It is easy to purchase equipment that is 'in vogue', without really considering whether it will help you to ride your horse more comfortably. The two main areas of sensitivity are the horse's mouth and his back.

Bits and bitting

This area is one of considerable debate. It is fair to say that problems with the rider's control of his horse often result from incorrect and inconsistent training. Many problems can also result from ill-fitting bits, that are uncomfortable in the horse's mouth. With correct discipline and some experimentation with different bits, a solution can often be found. However, you must first consider the structure of the horse's mouth and the action of common bits (**fig. 43**).

Pressure from a bit can be exerted on the bars, tongue and corners of the mouth (**fig. 44**). With some curb bits, pressure can also be exerted on the roof of the mouth, chin groove and poll.

(Opposite) **36** A correctly fitted tail bandage should finish about 1in (2.5cm) before the end of the dock

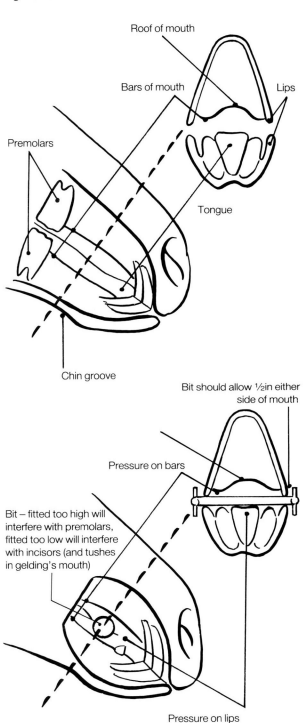

Fig. 43 Structure of the mouth

Roof of mouth

Bars of mouth

Lips

Premolars

Tongue

Chin groove

Bit should allow ½in either side of mouth

Pressure on bars

Bit – fitted too high will interfere with premolars, fitted too low will interfere with incisors (and tushes in gelding's mouth)

Pressure on lips
Some pressure on tongue

Fig. 44 Fitting a bit

Various materials can be used to make bits. Stainless steel is the best for general use, as it is hard-wearing and easy to clean. Various types of rubber, plastic and nylon may be used for horses with very sensitive mouths. Avoid nickel as it tends to wear sharp and can fracture.

The snaffle This can be of a very mild form, such as the half-moon snaffle, or very severe, such as the cherry roller. Most types of snaffle can be jointed or unjointed. The unjointed bit acts mainly on the bars of the mouth, and is mild, as extra pressure cannot easily be put on one side of the horse's mouth. The jointed snaffle allows you to exert pressure, with the so-called 'nutcracker' action (**fig. 45**). It is possible to put pressure on the corners of the mouth and, to a certain extent, on the tongue, as well as the bars. This makes it a more severe bit, and thus makes it easier to turn the horse, or make a one-sided horse more even in his contact. Snaffles are commonly either 'loose-ring' or 'eggbutt' (**37**). You will sometimes find that a horse that tends to be a little dead to the contact will work better in a loose ring, and a horse that is unsteady in his contact will work better in a eggbutt.

Curb bits There are many variations of these. For English riding, a curb bit is normally used as part of a double bridle (exceptions to this are Pelhams and kimblewicks), and the bit usually used is a Weymouth. Curb bits should always be used with the curb chain correctly fitted, or the chain may rub the horse (**fig. 46**). There are various types of curb chain. The metal chains are either single link (which are severe) or double link (which are milder). Some horses resent the feeling of the metal chain, so you may either put a rubber cover over the metal chain or use a chain which has leather inserted. It is also possible to purchase curb chains

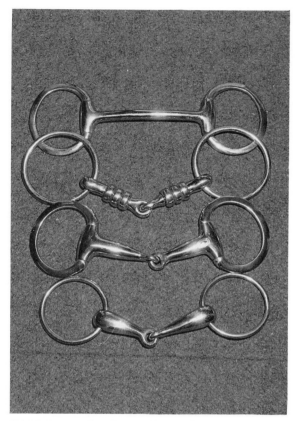

37 Mullen mouth, cherry-roller, eggbutt and loose ring snaffles

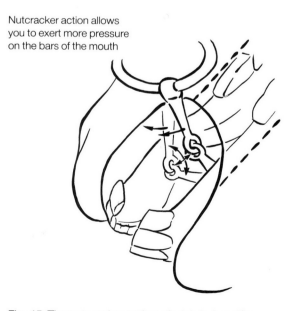

Nutcracker action allows you to exert more pressure on the bars of the mouth

Fig. 45 The nutcracker action of a jointed snaffle

with elastic inserted, but these are not permitted in competitions. The curb chain should be fitted so that it prevents the cheek of the bit from moving further than 45 degrees to the line of the mouth. Old-fashioned bits had a 'port' that acted on the roof of the horse's mouth, which made them very severe (**38**). Modern bits tend to have tongue grooves, that relieve the pressure on the tongue (**39**). Longer cheeks give more leverage, so are more severe. Curb bits provide more refinement and control, so should be used with a well-trained horse.

The Pelham Although this is a curb bit, it is classified separately, as it is on its own (unlike other curb bits). There are various types of Pelham, but they are all basically designed to give more control, so can be useful for jumping or hunting (**40**). Again, the severity depends upon the length of the cheek and the width of the mouth piece.

(Top right) **38** A Weymouth bit with a port

(Bottom right) **39** A Weymouth bit with a tongue groove

(Below) **40** A Pelham bit

Correctly fitted, curb chain should lie in the chin groove, preventing the cheek of the bit from moving more than 45 degrees

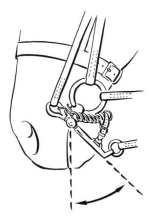

Fig. 46 Fitting a curb chain

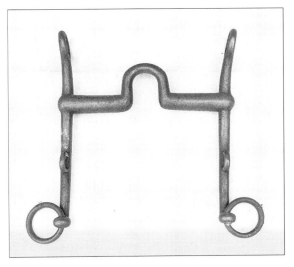

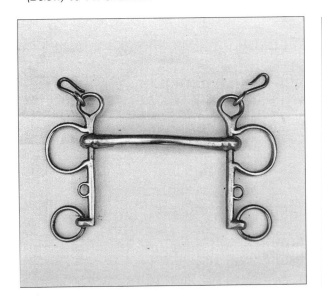

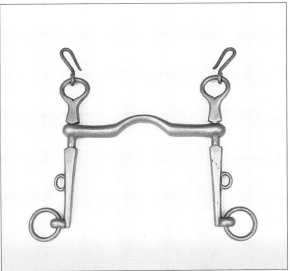

> If a horse is unhappy in his mouth, he will be difficult and uncomfortable to ride. The horse will flee from pain, so ill-fitting bits, sharp teeth, injury or poor training will all result in problems. The solution lies in remedying the cause, and *not* in choosing a more painful and worrying bit for the horse.

Bridles

The purpose of the bridle is the deciding factor on which design to buy. A fine-boned Thoroughbred will look better in a narrow leather bridle, whereas a cob looks better in thicker leather. The quality and thickness of the leather are major safety factors. Many pre-assembled bridles do not fit the horse correctly, so you must ensure that each piece of the bridle is the correct size (**41**).

Nosebands There are different types of noseband, ranging from the plain cavesson, fitted mostly for appearance, to the Kineton, which is designed to give more control. As a general rule, nosebands are used to prevent the horse from opening his mouth and resisting the contact: drop, Grackle (figure-eight) and flash nosebands are designed specifically for this purpose (**42, 43, 44**). It is very important that these nosebands are fitted correctly; often they either exert pressure in the wrong place, or are totally ineffective.

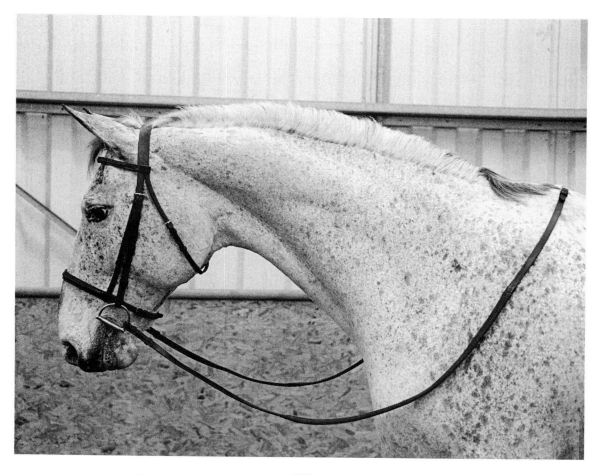

42 A correctly fitted drop noseband

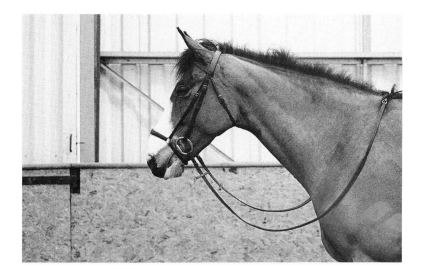

43 A correctly fitted flash noseband

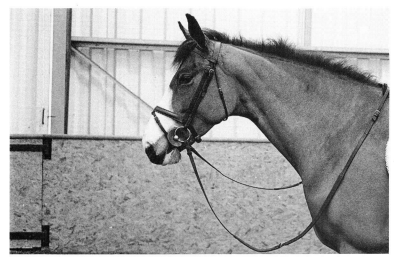

44 A correctly fitted Grackle (figure eight) noseband

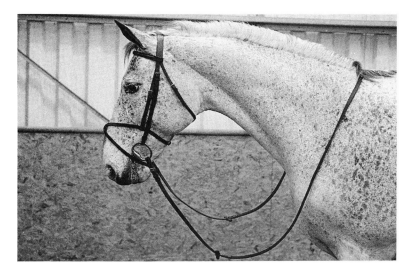

(Opposite) **41** A correctly fitted English bridle

The horse's spine, and saddle fitting

The horse's spine consists of seven cervical vertebrae, 18 thoracic vertebrae (each of which carries a pair of ribs), six lumbar vertebrae, a sacrum made of five bones fused together, and approximately 18 coccygeal (tail) vertebrae (**fig. 47**). Occasionally, and especially in Arabs, only five lumbar bones are present.

For saddle-fitting purposes the thoracic and lumbar vertebrae are of interest. The thoracic vertebrae are capable of very little movement, and have long spines that curve towards each other to form the withers. The lumbar vertebrae are long wide transverse processes, which project almost at right-angles to the spine.

The ribs The horse has 18 pairs of ribs, eight sternal (attached to the sternum), and ten asternal (attached to the spine, and to each other), the last rib is attached only to the spine, and is called a floating rib. The ribs protect the heart and lungs. They are moveable, thus allowing the horse to breath. Movement is restricted between and behind the shoulder blades.

The shoulder blades Each one attaches a foreleg to the trunk, by means of muscle. They lie over the first six or seven ribs, but are separated by muscles and connective tissue. The high degree of movement necessary in this area must not be restricted by the saddle.

The loins The loins stretch from the last rib back to the hips. They are the weakest part of the spine and should not be asked to support weight.

Types of saddle

There are many variations upon the basic design, but the common saddles used for English riding are the dressage, jumping and general purpose saddle.

Fig. 47 The horse's spine

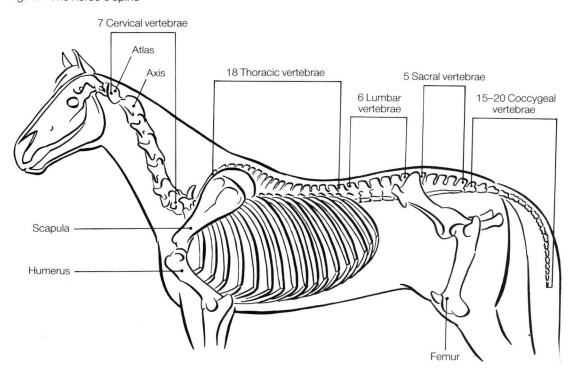

7 Cervical vertebrae

Atlas

Axis

18 Thoracic vertebrae

5 Sacral vertebrae

6 Lumbar vertebrae

15–20 Coccygeal vertebrae

Scapula

Humerus

Femur

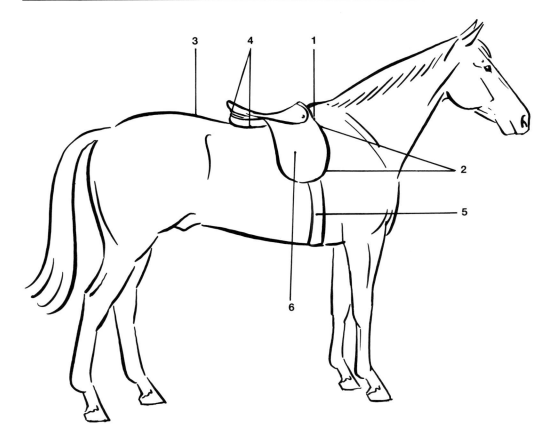

Fig. 48 Fitting a saddle

POINTS OF SADDLE FITTING

For all points see Fig. 48 above.

1 The withers must not be pinched or pressed upon.
2 The front part of the saddle must allow freedom of the shoulder blades.
3 The loins must bear no weight.
4 There must be an even weight distribution on each side of the back, with no pressure on the spine.
5 The saddle must allow the girth to lie in the girth groove.
6 The saddle must be of the correct size and shape for the rider.

The dressage saddle The straighter flap and shorter tree allow for a longer stirrup length (**45**). This allows more of the rider's leg to be in contact with the horse. This saddle is not good for hollow- or weak-backed horses, as it demands that they bear more of the rider's weight than other types of saddle.

The jumping saddle This is the complete opposite to the dressage saddle (**46**). Its longer tree and forward-cut flaps allow the rider to ride with shorter stirrups, and push his seat back to compensate for the more forward jumping position.

The general purpose saddle This is designed to be suitable for both dressage and jumping, although this aim is rarely achieved (**47**). It is however, suitable for general riding.

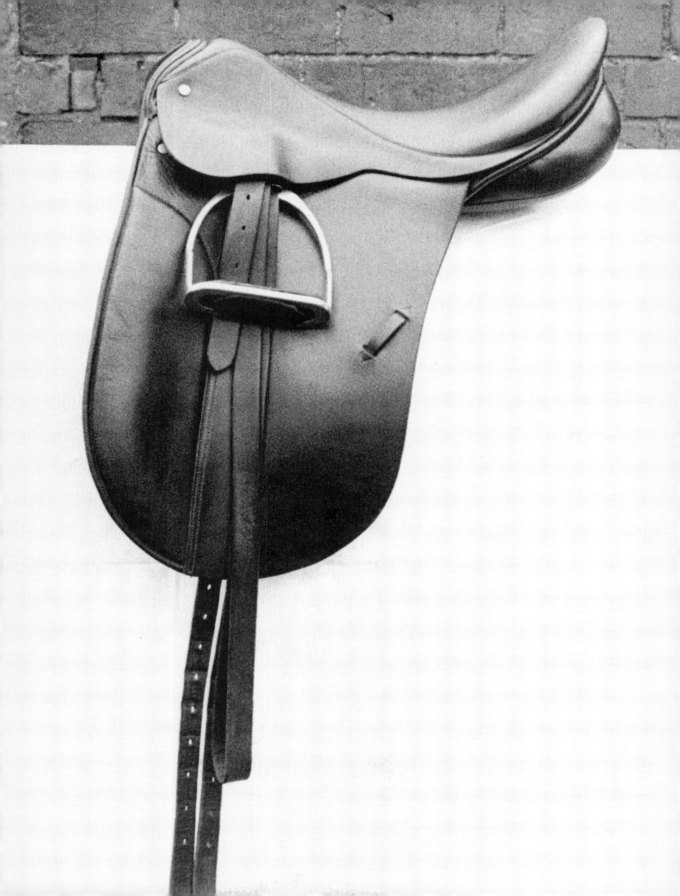

(Top right) **46** A jumping saddle

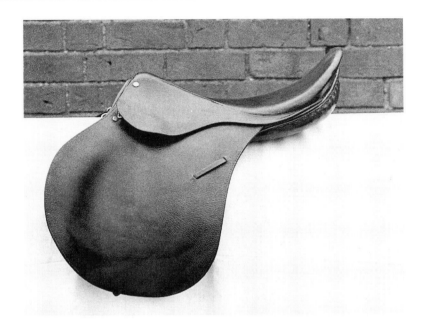

(Bottom right) **47** A general purpose (GP) saddle

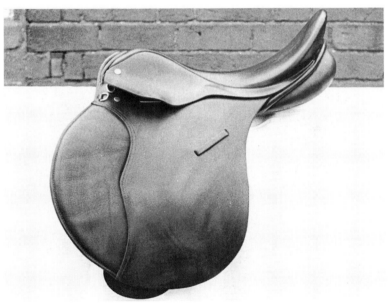

(Opposite) **45** A dressage saddle

Numnahs (saddle pads) Most modern saddles have leather linings, so must be fitted with a numnah, as tanned leather does not absorb sweat easily and therefore will rub. It is best to use cotton (or other natural fibre) numnahs. These absorb the sweat much better than synthetic materials. Traditionally, numnahs were used to make ill-fitting saddles fit the horse. However, a numnah cannot even out the distribution of the rider's weight, so problems will still occur. It is far better to use a correctly fitted saddle. There are many different types of numnahs and pads on the market, some, apparently, with therapeutic qualities. Basically, the more comfortable the horse is in its back, the better it will work.

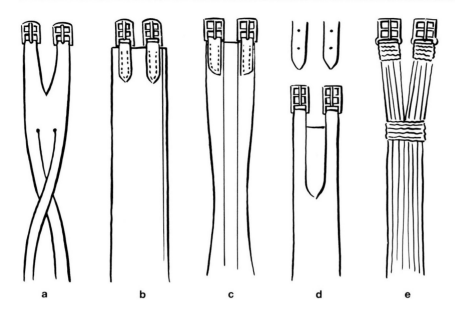

a **Leather balding** – cut to give freedom to elbows when galloping and to prevent rubbing

b **Three fold leather** – suitable for everyday use but not fast work

c **Atherstone** – usually leather, designed to give freedom to elbows

d **Lonsdale** – short girths for dressage saddles with long girth straps

e **String or nylon** – string are best, preventing rubbing by allowing air to girth region

a   b   c   d   e

Fig. 49 Girths in common use

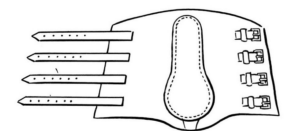

Leather/felt brushing boots – alternatives include plastic and nylon with various easy fastenings

Tendon boot – protects the tendons down back of leg from cuts/bruises due to hind feet

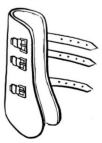

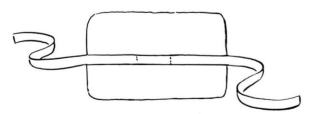

Yorkshire boot – felt, useful boot to protect fetlocks

Plastic or rubber over-reach boots – modern boots have easy fastenings

Fig. 50 Boots in common use

Girths The type of girth used will depend on the style of saddle, and on the type of work being done by the horse. Today, strong synthetic materials have replaced the more traditional leather girths, and they are certainly cheaper to buy and easier to care for. Whichever type of girth you choose, it must be of the correct length. Girths that are too short and have to be forced on will soon make the horse difficult to saddle. Girths that are too long will not secure the saddle enough, and so result in friction (**fig. 49**).

Boots Boots are often used to protect the ridden horse injuring itself (**fig. 50**). Particularly vulnerable areas are the inside of the lower limb, the fetlocks and heels. The causes of injury are varied:

some horses have faulty action due to poor conformation which effects the way they move, often knocking the opposite leg (brushing); others just lose their balance and catch their fore limb with their hind foot (over-reach). Young or untrained horses will be particularly vulnerable to injury when ridden as they will not be that well balanced. Horses are quite likely to injure themselves when they are tired as they will lose some of their co-ordination; particularly when competing cross-country, so boots or bandages are essential (they will also protect the horse's limbs if they knock the fences). The number of different types of boot available is considerable: synthetic materials are commonly used, and are as effective as traditional leather boots.

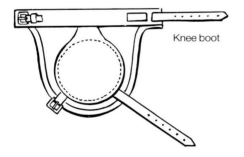

Knee boot

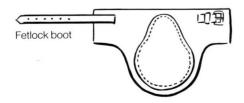

Fetlock boot

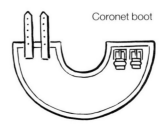

Coronet boot

SUMMARY

- Rugs should be well-fitting, light and warm.
- Bandages may be used to give warmth and protection.
- Saddlery must be correctly fitted, and a suitable design to be of comfort to both horse and rider.

11
CARE OF THE HORSE'S FEET

11
CARE OF THE HORSE'S FEET

Today, people realize that from infancy, we must buy shoes that are well-fitting, otherwise abnormalities and chronic conditions will develop, making it uncomfortable to walk. Athletes have a mass of technology behind their competition shoes to give them the best balance and performance. Yet many people still pay little regard to the condition of their horse's feet, waiting until the excessive hoof growth has loosened the shoes before calling the farrier. At speed, the horse will put up to 4000kg (9000lbs) on each foreleg. To cope with this the horn must be strong, necessitating a healthy diet. In addition, the foot must be in correct balance to the body, and the shoe should be the correct type for its purpose. The hooves must be checked daily to ensure that they are free from disease and damage.

The Structures of the Lower Limb and Hoof

The lower limb

The cannon bone This is the name given to the third metacarpal bone. It runs from the carpal bones of the knee, to the first phalanx, or long pastern bone. This bone takes a lot of weight when the horse is moving, so should be short in relation to the upper limb, for strength.

Splint bones These run down the back of the cannon, and are called the second and fourth metacarpal bones. They support the knee joint, bear weight from the body, and transfer it to the cannon bone.

Sesamoid bones These two bones form the back of the fetlock. They act as a fulcrum for the digital flexor tendons, and provide leverage for the suspensory apparatus.

The long pastern This is also known as the first phalanx. It runs from the cannon bone to the short pastern (second phalanx) at an angle of about 50 degrees. The lateral digital extensor attaches to this bone.

The short pastern This is also known as the second phalanx. The superficial flexor tendon is attached to this bone.

The pedal bone Sometimes referred to as the coffin bone, this is the third phalanx. It is made up of very dense bone, through which many blood vessels run. The common digital extensor tendon attaches to the front of the bone, and the deep flexor tendon attaches to the underside.

The pedal bone is suspended in place by the medial and lateral cartilages, which extend above the coronet.

The navicular bone This is another sesamoid bone. It is situated behind the joint of the short pastern and pedal bones. It acts as a fulcrum for the deep digital flexor tendons.

Ligaments These connect bone to bone (**fig. 52**). In the lower limb, they determine the way a joint moves and help support the joint.

Suspensory ligament This extends from the carpal bones of the knee, and runs down between the cannon bone and the deep digital flexor tendon. At the felock it divides, part of it running behind the fetlock and over the sesamoid bones, and the other part running down to the toe of the pedal bone. This ligament's main function is to support and control the movement of the fetlock joint.

Check ligaments Also known as accessory ligaments, these support the lower leg. One joins the deep digital flexor to the cannon bone below the knee, and the other joins the superficial flexor tendon to the radius above the knee.

The tendons There is no muscle below the knee and hock of the horse. The tendons are extensions of the flexor and extensor muscles.

Digital extensor tendons There are two of these. The common digital extensor runs down the front of the leg and attaches to the pedal bone. The lateral digital extensor runs down the side of the leg and attaches to the long pastern bone.

Digital flexor tendons The deep flexor tendon runs behind the suspensory ligament and down into the hoof over the sesamoid and navicular bones, attaching to the underside of the pedal bone. The superficial flexor tendon runs behind the

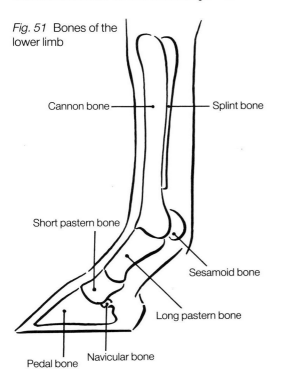

Fig. 51 Bones of the lower limb

Cannon bone — — Splint bone

Short pastern bone

Sesamoid bone

Long pastern bone

Pedal bone — Navicular bone

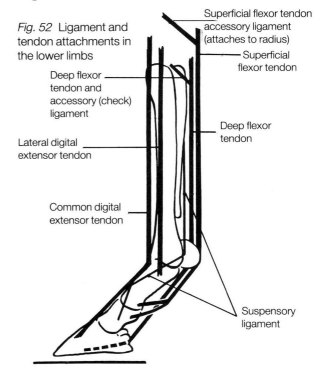

Fig. 52 Ligament and tendon attachments in the lower limbs

Superficial flexor tendon accessory ligament (attaches to radius)

Superficial flexor tendon

Deep flexor tendon and accessory (check) ligament

Deep flexor tendon

Lateral digital extensor tendon

Common digital extensor tendon

Suspensory ligament

deep flexor tendon, and over the sesamoid bones, where it divides to attach to either side of the short pastern.

The hoof

Horn This is a modified form of skin, having a tougher, thicker form of epidermis (**fig. 53**). Different types of horn make up the wall, sole and frog.

The wall This bears most of the horse's weight. It consists of three layers: the periople, the tubular horn layer, and the insensitive laminae.

The periople is made up of a thin layer of tubular horn that grows down from the perioplic band. It acts as a waterproofing layer.

The tubular horn layer grows down from the papillae of the coronary band and consists of parallel horn tubules, cemented together by intertubular horn.

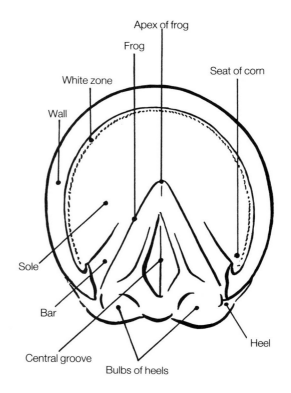

Fig. 54 The underside of the hoof

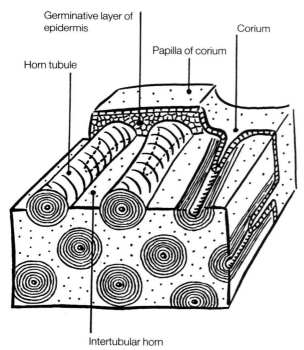

Fig. 53 The structure of horn

The insensitive laminae interlocks with the sensitive laminae, joining the wall to the pedal bone.

The wall and bars provide a bearing surface, with the bars supporting the heels (**fig. 54**).

The sole This is concaved, to allow the wall and frog to bear the horse's weight. The insensitive sole is made up of short horn tubules that grow from the papillae of the sensitive sole. The sensitive sole joins to the periosteum (outer membrane) of the pedal bone. Where the insensitive sole joins the insensitive wall, a white line appears, which acts as a guide to farriers.

The frog This was once thought to be the 'pump' of the foot, driving blood back up the leg. It does have a slight pumping effect, although it is now known that it is the whole weight of the horse that drives

the de-oxygenated blood back up the veins of the leg. The frog provides some grip, the cleft giving security over unlevel going. The insensitive frog is made of horn, which grows from the papillae of the sensitive frog. Above that is the digital cushion, which helps support the pedal bone and provides protection for the navicular bone and the deep flexor tendon, which passes over the navicular bone, before attaching to the underside of the pedal bone. The frog, along with the digital cushion, does have a 'cushioning' effect when the hoof bears weight, and this helps to alleviate some of the concussion.

Correct foot balance

Correct foot balance refers to the foot being the correct shape to enable weight to be borne evenly on all the joints of the leg and, anatomically, starts at the shoulder (**fig. 55**). Few horses have a perfectly shaped foot.

Obtaining the correct foot balance is vital to the performance of the domesticated horse, and we rely on the farrier to trim the horse's foot correctly. The hoof grows about 1cm (⅜in) a month, so the shod horse should receive attention about once a month. A common mistake is to not trim the toe sufficiently, and so put too much weight on the heel (**figs. 56, 57**).

This can start a vicious circle as the pressure on the heel restricts hoof growth, causing the toe to grow faster.

Good farriery

A good farrier should first balance the horse's foot. Next he must choose the correct size, shape, and type of shoe and fit it correctly. Few farriers now shoe 'tight to the heel', recognizing the need to give support to the heel (**figs. 58, 59**).

Nails These should be driven home, and should not be knocked into old nail holes.

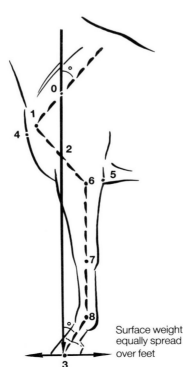

Fig. 55 The slope of the hoof should equal the slope of the shoulder and pastern. The hoof should support the horse's weight evenly

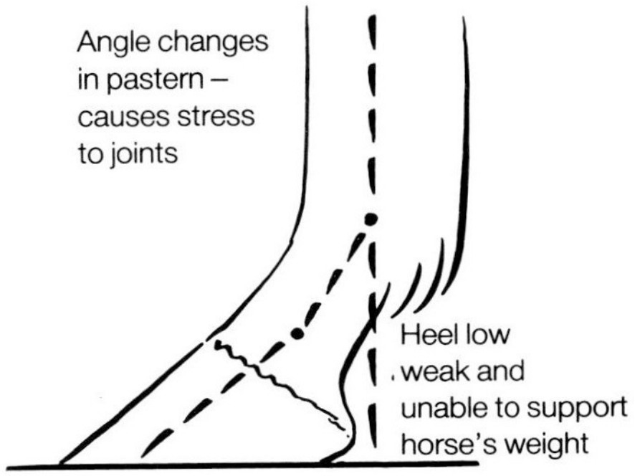

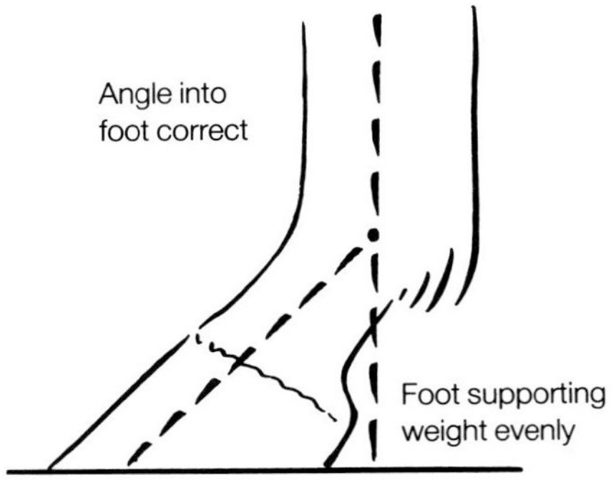

Fig. 56 Toes and heels: long toes and weak heels will cause serious problems

Fig. 57 A correctly balanced foot

Surface weight equally spread over feet

Angle changes in pastern – causes stress to joints

Heel low, weak and unable to support horse's weight

Angle into foot correct

Foot supporting weight evenly

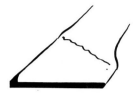

Fig. 58 Foot shod tight to the heel

Fig. 59 Foot shod to support the heel

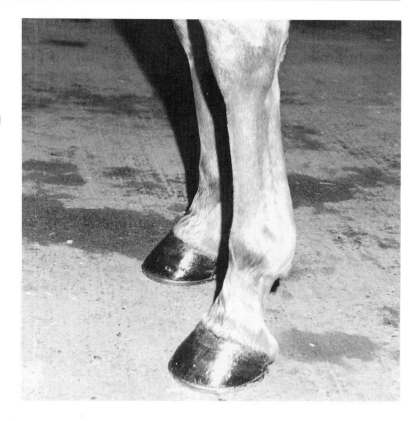

(Right) **48** A well-shod foot

If they are knocked in too low (fine nailing) the shoe will fall off; too high (coarse nailing) and they may enter the sensitive part of the foot, causing lameness.

Toe clips These should be good and broad to spread the pressure as the horse pushes against them.

Rasping This should not be excessive, or it will weaken the horn. All sharp edges should be rasped so the horse cannot damage himself (**48**).

Studs These are used to give added grip when working on and off the road. There are different types of stud; some are used for road work (**fig. 66**) and some for work-

ing on grass (**fig. 67**). The farrier will 'tap' a hole in the back of the shoe, into which the stud is screwed (**fig. 68**). Care should be taken to fill the hole with cotton wool when it is not being used.

SUMMARY

- Horses must receive attention from the farrier every four to six weeks, even if unshod.
- A well-shod foot will be correctly balanced to the horse's body.
- It may be necessary with some horses to use special shoes to prevent injury or aid recovery from disease.

In order, top to bottom and left to right:

Fig. 60 A hunter shoe with calkin and wedge: concaved to lighten the shoe and to prevent it being pulled off in mud. The calkin and wedge on the back pair give extra grip

Fig. 61 A broad web shoe: reduces concussion and gives support, so a good shoe for flat footed horses. It may be plain stamp (no fullering), or fullered

Fig. 62 A feather edge shoe: used for horses that brush. The shoe is rounded on the inside, on the part of the shoe that would strike the other foreleg

Fig. 63 A diamond toe shoe: used for horses that forge (strike the outside of the front shoe with the hind shoe)

Fig. 64a–c Bar shoes come in different patterns, but are basically designed to give support to weak heels

Fig. 64a An egg bar shoe

Fig. 64b A heart bar shoe

Fig. 64c A bar shoe

Fig. 65 A pattern shoe: used in cases of strained tendons. This relieves pressure on the tendons while they heal

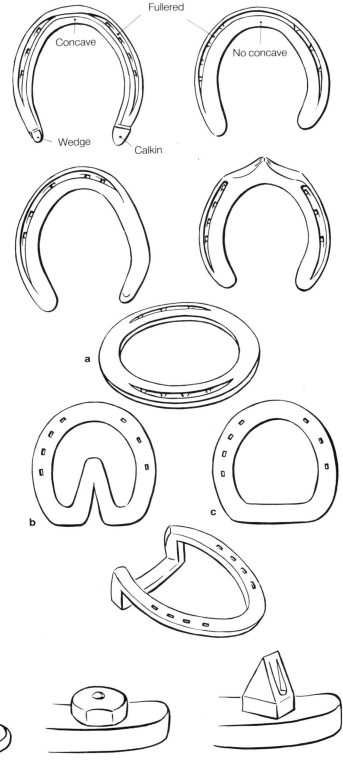

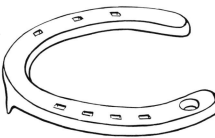

Fig. 66 Stud holes

Fig. 67 Road stud fitted

Fig. 68 Jumping stud fitted

12
TRAVELLING

12
TRAVELLING

It will almost certainly be necessary, at some time, to transport your horse away from home. This may be a regular occurrence, to hunt or compete: or an occasional journey to the vet, or for a lesson. Journeys can be made by land, sea or air.

Before you travel you must make routine checks and preparations to help ensure a problem-free journey. Remember that travelling is stressful to the horse, particularly if it occurs only occasionally, so precautions will need to be taken before, during, and after the journey.

The Vehicle

You will normally either transport the horse by trailer or lorry. Routine checks to the vehicles should be made monthly, it is no use checking everything the day before, as it may be difficult to get any mechanical work done, or obtain parts in the event of problems.

Routine checks

Check that the tyres have enough air, and are in good condition. This is particularly important if you carry heavy loads. Trailers tend to stand around a lot, and their tyres perish. This can make them very dangerous, as the tyres may split under the weight of a horse, even at slow speeds.

The lorry or vehicle pulling the trailer must be taxed and insured as required.

Check that the vehicle has plenty of oil, fuel, etc., and that all electrics work.

Check that the floor is sound and not rotten, and if the vehicle has been stood around for a while, it is a good idea to check that the brakes have not seized up before you set off!

Equipment

If you are travelling to a competition, remember to pack all the equipment you will need throughout the competition. If you plan to be away for a night, or a few days, you need to pack enough of your horse's usual feed and bedding, and water, if it will not be available on-site. For long journeys, it is essential that you pack extra feed and water to give your horse at stopping points during the journey, and possibly a change of rugs in case he sweats up. Horses can travel for up to 48 hours on long journeys abroad, and will survive quite happily, as long as they are fed and watered regularly. Obviously, you can take as much as you want, but a simple list, such as given below, should be enough for most occasions.

TRAVELLING LIST

- Simple equine and human first-aid kits.
- Feed, hay and water. It is better to take your own supply to be sure of not contaminating the horse (remember your buckets).
- Bedding and mucking-out tools, if staying away.
- Tack and equipment required. It is a good idea to take spares of the vital elements, such as girths and reins.
- All documentation required for the horse. Some countries require an FEI passport.

This is an international passport that is issued by the International Equestrian Federation. It identifies the horse and gives a record of its vaccinations and the nationality of owner and horse.

- A sweat sheet, or cooler sheet, and a change of rugs.
- It is simpler to have a travel box with most of the grooming kit, studs, first-aid kits, etc. already in it!
- Rider's clothes if required.

49 Dressed for travelling with shipping boots

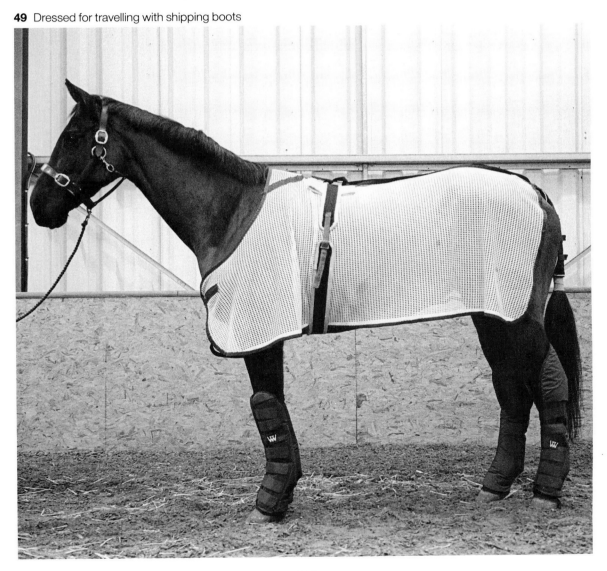

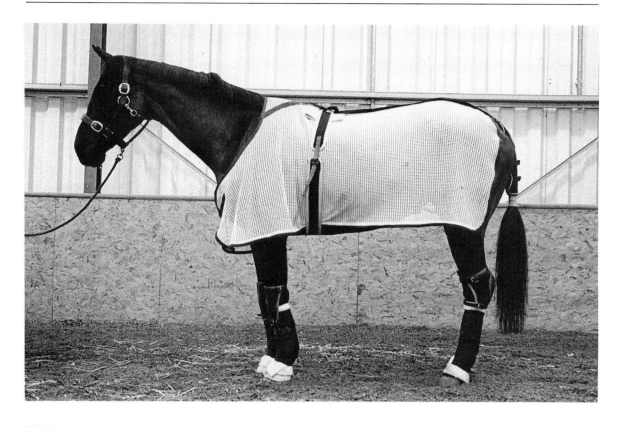

Preparing the Horse

Some people will pad their horse from head to foot to travel, whilst others use little more than a headcollar. It is certainly a matter of preference, but the following equipment covers the basics.

Headcollar This should preferably be leather, as nylon can cut and burn the horse behind the ears if he pulls back. The rope should have either a quick-release mechanism, or be of natural fibres, so that it will break if strained badly. It is certainly better that the rope breaks and not the horse's neck!

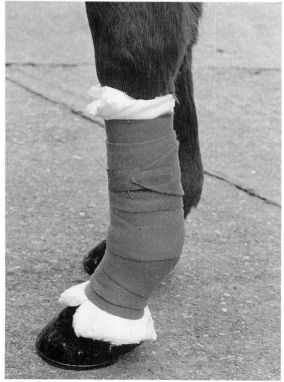

(Top) **50** Dressed for travelling with bandages, knee, hock and over-reach boots

51 Travel bandages offer more protection than stable bandages, especially around the bulbs of the heels

Poll guard This is certainly advisable if you are transporting the horse in a vehicle with a low roof. If you do not have a poll guard, even wrapping cloth around the top of the headcollar helps.

Rugs The horse should wear the equivalent weight of what he wears in the stable. If he tends to sweat up, you may replace a rug with a sweat sheet. It is very important, particularly when transporting the horse in a trailer, that the horse has some type of rug to protect him from the partition or any protrusion.

Leg protection You can use either traditional travel bandages, with knee, hock and over-reach boots for added protection, or in the new all-in-one shipping boots (**49**). The horse should certainly have some kind of protection, particularly around the heels, from treads from himself or by other horses (**50, 51**).

Tail protection This is vital, especially if the horse is resting against the tail-board of a trailer, as he can rub his tail raw in a very short time. There are many different types of tail guard on the market, but even two tail bandages, applied one on top of the other, will help.

Loading

Some thought must be given to the horse's psychology before attempting to load. Position the box or trailer where it will encourage him to go up the ramp; alongside a wall or in a gateway can be helpful. It is also better not to load the horse away from his stable companions. Always allow plenty of time for loading and the journey – neither you nor the horse want any extra stress. It towing a trailer, check that the hitch is safe and correct before you load (**52**).

52 Check that the trailer is safely hitched. There should be a chain or wire attached to the brake, in case the trailer comes away from the hitch

LOADING TIPS

- Position the vehicle so that the horse has no escape routes when loading.
- Check that the ramp is stable. A horse will be very reluctant to walk up an unsteady ramp.
- Have an assistant to help you if you think that the horse may be difficult.
- Always wear gloves, particularly with a strange horse, as you may get rope burns if he pulls away from you.
- If possible, move the partition to give the horse plenty of room to load **(53)**.
- When the horse has loaded, lift the ramp from the side. Try not to stand directly behind the ramp, as you may get trampled if the horse rushes back.
- Park the vehicle in a place that will encourage the horse to load **(53)**.

Difficult horses The horse that will not load is every horse owner's nightmare. However, it can quite often be just because the trailer roof is too low, or the box too dark. Some horses will be genuinely frightened, and simply need gentle coaxing; the majority will probably need no more than a slap on the hind-quarters. Lunge lines can be used to help load horses (**54**); bridles also give more control, if you expect trouble.

54 Lunge lines should be securely attached to the trailer, and crossed behind the horse

The journey

Over a long journey, it will be necessary to stop and give the horse feed and water, and to check his rugs. Some horses may need to be unloaded and walked for a few moments to allow them to urinate. Sensible and careful driving will help ensure that you do not overstress your horse en route.

Remember that he will be using his strength to balance, which can be quite tiring, so avoid rapid cornering, or heavy braking.

After the Journey

Travelling, particularly for more than three hours, is very stressful for the horse, particularly if he has been competing as well. Proper aftercare is very important, and the horse should be treated just as if he has done a strenuous day's work.

On arrival home, unload the horse, and walk him in-hand for ten to fifteen minutes, to encourage him to stretch and relax his muscles.

Next, tie the horse up in the stable, and remove his travelling equipment. Check him over for injury. Then untie the horse, give him the opportunity to roll, and offer him a drink. Re-rug him, and give him a haynet, and a small feed.

Unload the vehicle and muck it out. Be careful to remove all wet bedding, to prevent the floor from rotting.

Check the horse an hour later, and last thing at night to be sure that he is comfortable. Change the rugs if necessary.

The day after a long journey, or a competition, it is important that you trot the horse up to check that he is sound, and to thoroughly inspect again for injury. You may lightly exercise the horse, or turn him out in the field for a short while.

Other Methods of Transporting Horses

Horses travel by air and sea to compete abroad or when being imported to a new country. It is best to employ specialist firms to ship the horses and deal with all the necessary paperwork involved. They will also advise you on which blood tests the horse must have taken to check that he is free from disease, and arrange for a vet to examine the horse before it is transported to give it a certificate of health.

SUMMARY

- Routine checks must be made to the vehicle for safety.
- Allow adequate time to prepare the horse and equipment.
- Load the horse in a place that will encourage it to go up the ramp.
- Over a long journey, check the horse at least every two hours.
- After a long journey, the horse must be treated with care.

Part 3
TURNING THE HORSE AWAY TO GRASS

13

CORRECT CARE OF GRASSLAND

Grass is the most natural foodstuff for the horse, and if of good quality, it is nutritious as well as filling. Grass keeps the horse's gut healthy and is one of the most economical forms of feed. However, the very nature of the beast does not lend itself to the maintenance of good quality grassland; horses churn it up with their cone-like feet, they waste large areas of grassland by soiling it, and if not monitored will graze the grass to the roots. Most horse owners are limited in the amount of grassland that they have available. This tends to magnify the above problems, and therefore intensively grazed land needs special care, if it is not to become an area of weed-infested, parasite-ridden, poor-quality grassland.

The Feed Value of Grass

The older the grass sward is, the more fibrous and less digestible it becomes. Grass is most nutritious in its young growing stage, around May and early June. By August it has become dry and fibrous, because as the grass matures, the cell walls surrounding the nutritious cell contents become thicker, and the cell contents smaller. The cell walls are made from cellulose, polysaccharides and lignin. Lignin is particularly indigestible, and also prevents other nutrients from being easily digested. The cell contents are made up from proteins, simple sugars, lipids and minerals.

Grass species

Perennial rye This is the most commonly used grass, as it has played an important role in agriculture for many years, and is a nutritious grass that grows well in medium to high soil fertility (55). There are, to date, 34 different varieties, and some are more favoured by horses than others. However, this particular variety suffers from cold winters, and growth will be delayed if the spring is cold.

Hybrid ryegrass This is a mixture of strains of perennial ryegrass with the more nutritious Italian ryegrass, that is now favoured by farmers. The hybrid combines the high nutritional value of the Italian rye with the longer growing season of the perennial rye.

Timothy This is another popular grass, although for horses, it is not the most nutritional because it tends to be high in lignin (55). It is at its most nutritious early in the season, and makes a good hay crop if cut early.

(From the left)
55 Perennial rye, timothy, cocksfoot and meadow fescue

Cocksfoot This is the least digestible of the commonly used grasses **(55)**. It is a hardy plant, but horses tend to find it unpalatable.

Fescues Meadow fescues, in particular, have been found to make good mixes with the hardier grasses, such as perennial rye **(55)**. They are still fairly nutritious on less fertile soil, so are a useful crop.

Soil

There are many different soil types. The fertility and productivity of soil is determined by its mineral content, its acidity, the temperature, and the amount of light and water available.

Soil contains the minerals potassium, phosphorus, magnesium, sulphur, and other trace elements. Nitrogen plays an important part in the soil's fertility, and

organic matter makes up the bulk of the soil. Soil types are governed by the bedrock on which they grow. Soil fertility is dependant on the availability of all the necessary constituents, particularly the major minerals – potassium and phosphorus. The temperature is governed by the seasons, and by the situation of the grassland. Higher slopes may be colder, so therefore less productive. The amount of light will also be seasonal, the longer days of spring and early summer being the most productive. The fertility of the soil will affect the growth rate of the grass, and any nutritional deficiencies will be passed on to the horse.

Routine Care of Grassland

Fertilizers

Fertilizers help to maintain a good, healthy crop of grass, even in adverse growing conditions. The soil should first of all be analysed to determine the correct balance of nutrients required. There are many different fertilizers available, but they generally fall into one of two main categories; organic and inorganic.

Organic Traditional farmyard manure is the most popular organic fertilizer. It tends to be rich in a wide range of nutrients, and contains the necessary nitrogen, phosporus and potassium. However, like many of the organic fertilizers, it is slow to rot down and dissolve into the soil. This may cause problems, especially if you are unable to keep the horses off the land any length of time. Manure is often put down during late autumn, to allow enough time for it to rot into the soil. Other organic fertilizers include seaweed, kelp and chicken manure. Human sewage and pig manure are not advisable because of their high metal contents.

Inorganic These can either be compounded together to form a mixture, or be straight fertilizers. They are refined in a factory and the compounded fertilizers are mixed to form different balances, e.g. nitrogen: phospate: potash 20:10:10. This means that you can buy the correct balance for your particular soil, depending on the soil analysis. Straight fertilizer, such as nitrogen, can be bought, but this is usually bought by farmers to speed up the growth rate of the grass. These straight fertilizers are often applied at the beginning of the growth season, around the end of March. They are fast-acting, which can cause problems with horses, as the lush growth of nitrogen-rich grass can cause metabolic imbalances and disorders.

Lime Although this is a type of fertilizer, it has to be mentioned on its own, as its main constituent, calcium, has an important effect on the growth rate of the grass. Sandy soils need to have lime put down at least every three to four years, as the rain washes it away. Clay soils, however, will probably require it less often. It is very useful on acidic land as it raises the pH level.

Rolling

Horses tend to destroy grassland by churning it up, and this causes a number of problems. Where the horse cuts up the grass, weeds can grow, also, the holes can fill with water and affect the drainage of the soil. When the soil is dry, the uneven footing can cause the horse to trip and stumble. Rolling the soil helps stop all these problems, and also provides a firmer consistency to the soil, which will help grass growth. However, if the ground is compounded too much, it will damage the structure of the soil, so care must be taken when rolling.

Harrowing

This is an essential part of grassland management. Harrowing spreads the horse's droppings, and so prevents areas becoming very horse-sick, and it also helps by pulling up the dead roots of grass in the spring, allowing the new season's shoots through.

Topping

This is the term used when you use a grass cutter to 'top' the grass when it has become very long. It is particularly useful with horse pasture, as horses do not like to eat grass that has grown longer than 13–15cm (5–6in).

Topping is also a good means of control-

a Ragwort (*Senecio jacobaea*)

d Bracken (*Pteridium aquilinum*)

Fig. 69 Common weeds

b Buttercup (*Ranunculus repens*)

c Foxglove (*Digitalis purpurea*)

ling weed infestation, if done regularly, and is more environment-friendly than herbicides. It is often done through July and August, but should be done as often as necessary to keep the grass in good order.

Weed control

This is an important activity, which is often neglected. Weeds are very hardy plants, that will soon establish themselves and reduce the growing area available to the grass. Many weeds thrive in the more acidic soils, so are predominate in horse-sick pasture. With good management, they will often disappear as the grassland improves. Some weeds are poisonous, so need treating with special care. There are various ways of dealing with weeds (**fig. 69**).

Herbicides These are chemicals that are sprayed directly on to the weed, usually at the height of the growing season, between April and May. They are usually chemical hormones that kill the young, growing plant. Although herbicides can kill the grass too, you can buy selective herbicides that will kill only broad-leaf plants. All stock should be kept off the land for a couple of weeks to allow the weeds to die, and the herbicide to be dispersed.

However, if poisonous plants are present, the horses should not be returned to the land until they have disintegrated, as they are often readily eaten in their wilted state. For this reason, the use of herbicides to control poisonous plants is often impractical for the horse owner with limited land.

Topping As mentioned above, this can be an effective way of controlling weeds if done regularly. However, it is only effective if used as part of a correct manage-

ment programme. Again, if poisonous plants are present, care must be taken to remove all parts of the weed.

Hand-pulling This is very labour-intensive and unnecessary for the majority of weeds. However, with poisonous weeds, particularly ragwort, it is the safest and most effective way of eradication.

Common poisonous plants

Not only is it necessary for the horse's well-being to remove these, it is also necessary by law. The Weeds Act of 1959 requires that landowners eradicate certain listed undesirable weeds from their grassland.

Parasite control

Parasites that invade and damage the horse's digestive tract are called endoparasites (see Chapter 5). The larvae of these endoparasites crawl up the short blades of grass and are swallowed by the horse. Much can be done to reduce these life-threatening parasites, firstly by a controlled worming programme for the horse, and secondly by careful management of the grassland.

Removal of Dung Parasites are spread via the horse's dung, from which they migrate into the surrounding pasture. Even horses that are regularly wormed will infect the grassland to a certain degree. Removal of the horse's dung will help, and should be done daily on intensively grazed land. On larger areas of land, harrowing helps, although it is said that you will only kill the larvae by harrowing if the sun is baking hot. Harrowing also helps to spread the manure, and so prevent particular areas of the land becoming horse-sick.

Cross-grazing Cross-grazing cattle or sheep with the horse on your land, helps to reduce the worm burden as the equine endoparasites cannot survive the digestive tracts of the other species. The only problem with this system is that horse fencing may not safely contain sheep or cattle, so temporary additional fencing may be necessary.

Making hay Larvae cannot survive for long on long grass, so making hay from the pasture helps to kill them off. However, horse pasture rarely makes hay of a good enough quality for horses. In addition, unless you have your own machinery, it is not really practical to make it yourself anyway. You may be able to sell the crop of grass to a local farmer, who will use it to make hay for his sheep or cattle.

Stocking rates

This depends on the quality of the land, but, roughly, you should have 0.4–0.6 hectares (1–1½ acres) per horse. Most people have to make do with less land than that, but you will find it difficult to keep the horse healthy on more intensively grazed land, without supplementing his feed. Intensively grazed land requires very careful management to ensure good quality grass, a low worm burden and maximum grass coverage.

SUMMARY

- Grass is a valuable source of nutrition.
- Careful management will ensure maximum land usage.
- Parasite infestation will be reduced by correct management.

14
TURNING THE STABLED HORSE AWAY TO GRASS

14

TURNING THE STABLED HORSE AWAY TO GRASS

The End of the Season

At the end of the season, or at some time during the year, you may wish to turn your stabled horse away to grass. The careful preparations discussed in Chapter 2 now have to be applied in reverse. After a season in the stable, you have acclimatized the horse to this environment. Now you wish to turn him away, and must make his change into a field-kept horse a gradual process, to allow him time to adapt.

Finding a happy medium

The merits of giving the horse a period of rest at grass are open to discussion. It is good to turn the horse out for a period, but it is unhealthy to allow him to run to fat, so he should be lightly worked, during his time at grass, or his grazing controlled by keeping him in the stable for part of the day. However, most establishments turn their horses away at the end of their particular season, to give their staff a well earned rest, so to continue working the horses is out of the question. As with all things, a happy medium can be found, and by using your discretion it should be possible to give the horse a short break without allowing him to become unhealthy and obese.

Preparing to Turn the Horse Away

The field

As discussed in Chapter 13, the grassland must be well cared for, and of good quality.

Fencing This must be secure. There is some debate as to the best type of fencing for horses. Traditional post-and-rail is certainly one of the safest and most attractive forms of fencing, but also one of the most expensive. Smooth wire can be quite successful, if it is kept at the correct tension, but is dangerous if loose, and also should have a top rail or something similar, as a horse may not see the plain strand, and this could lead to a horrible accident if the horse tries to gallop through it. Electric fencing is becoming increasingly popular, as it is fairly inexpensive and allows you to divide your fields as you wish, in order to graze them more effectively. If your field is surrounded by a hedge, some form of fencing will still be necessary as horses will either push their way or eat through it.

Gates These should be hung so that they swing easily. It can be difficult and dangerous to get horses out of a field if the

gate is heavy and difficult to move. With the problems today of horse theft, all gates should be padlocked, and the top hinge turned upside down (**fig. 70**).

Water supply There are few streams that are clean enough for horses to drink from. It is far better to fence the stream off and provide an alternative water supply. The most efficent and economical system is the self-filling water trough. Whichever system you use, the trough must have no sharp edges, and be secured so that the horse cannot knock it over. It should be situated away from the corners of the field, as horses may trap each other behind it or stop more timid horses from getting to the water. It is also better to situate the trough away from trees and bushes, as the falling leaves will quickly rot in the water.

Field shelter It is important the field-kept horse has some form of shelter to protect him from the elements. In the winter, the wind and rain can make his life miserable and, in the summer, so will the sun and the flies. The shelter should be large enough to accommodate the number of horses in the field. Horses can bully each other quite badly, so the open-fronted type of shelter is better, with its back corners rounded off to prevent horses getting trapped.

The horse

The term commonly used for preparing the horse to be turned away is 'roughing off', and you should allow at least three weeks to accustom the horse to living out.

Feeding The concentrate feed should be cut down simultaneously with the exercise. As you cut the concentrate, increase the hay ration to compensate. Much depends on what time of year you turn the horse out, but if it is in the spring, the horse should be turned out for an hour or two a day in the first week, to accustom him to the rich grass. In any case, the horse should be turned out for a short while each day to compensate for the reduction in exercise. It is better, the first few times out, to ride the horse, and then turn him out hungry, so that he is too busy eating to gallop around.

Fig. 70 Gate hinges: turn the top hinge upside-down to prevent the gate being lifted off

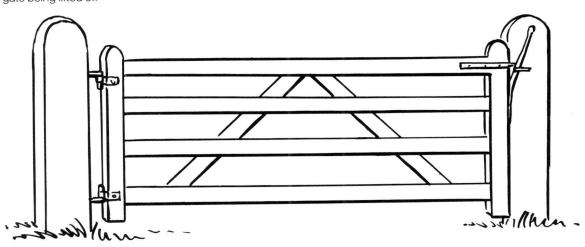

Exercise This can be reduced fairly quickly over the first week. As you begin cutting the feed, reduce the exercise; probably to half an hour by the end of the week. By this time the horse should be going out during the day to grass.

Grooming The thorough cleaning of the horse (strapping) should cease, to allow his body grease to build up, as this grease is the horse's protection against the elements. The daily care of the feet, eyes, nose and dock must continue, even when the horse is living out in the field.

Rugging Again, this depends on the time of year that the horse is turned out. If the horse is clipped out, he will still need rugging up if the weather is cold. Ideally, you should reduce the rugs the horse wears over the three weeks, but the horse may require a New Zealand rug to protect him in the field even after three weeks. If the weather is mild and warm, rugs can be dispensed with fairly quickly.

Turning out period This should be gradually increased over the three weeks until the horse is out completely, or out all day and in during the night. As mentioned before, it may be too cold to turn the horse away completely.

Shoeing As discussed in Chapter 2, if your farrier agrees it is a good idea to remove the horse's shoes to allow his feet to expand. However, some horses' feet will not stand up to this, as they require the support of the shoes to stop them splitting.

Traditionally, horses were fitted with 'grass tips' when they were roughed off, but this is not commonly done now. It is, however, a good idea to remove the back shoes on all the turned-out horses, to prevent them damaging each other.

Companions Horses thrive in each other's company, so a companion is important. However, it is not a good idea to turn mares and geldings out together, as they tend to fight, particularly if the mares out-number the geldings. You will soon learn which horses go with which; some horses are tremendous bullys, and will attack timid horses, but be perfectly well behaved when put out with bolder companions.

Caring for the Horse at Grass

You should check the horse at least once daily. If he is rugged, or requires feeding, you may need to check him up to three times each day.

Daily check

Each day, you should first check that all the horses are all there that should be there. One at a time, approach and put a headcollar on each horse, pick out his feet, look over for cuts or injury, and trot out for a few steps to see that he is sound.

Then release the horse, and have a good look around the field for any litter or other objects that may be deposited there.

Check the fencing, gates and water. Then check the field shelter, and, if necessary, skip it out.

Finally check that there is adequate grazing, and if not, feed.

Routine care

Whilst the horse is out at grass, he should receive regular attention from the farrier, and be wormed every six weeks. Although there is less daily work involved in keeping the horse at grass, careful observation and correct care of the pasture are still required to ensure the horse's continued good health.

Preparing for the Next Season

Note that most of the preparations for the next season must be initiated as soon as the horse is turned away (see Chapter 2).

SUMMARY

- Turning away the stabled horse is a gradual process, and should be done with care.
- Careful management of the field and the field-kept horse is required to maintain good health.
- Prepare for the next season as much as possible whilst the horse is still out.

CHECK LIST

- The stables should be cleared out and disinfected.
- Repairs should be made to the buildings as necessary, to make them sound and safe.
- All rugs should be cleaned, repaired and stored, with mothballs.
- All tack should be cleaned, and repaired if necessary, and stored.
- The clipping machine should be serviced and its blades sharpened, and stored away in a dry place.
- A general and thorough 'spring clean' of the yard, feed-room and tack room should be made.

APPENDIX I

APPENDIX II

BIBLIOGRAPHY

EQUESTRIAN SUPPLIERS & FURTHER STUDY

GLOSSARY

INDEX

APPENDIX I
CARE OF THE HORSE WHEN COMPETING

For many people, competing is the reward for the time and money spent caring for their horse. The added bonus is to win or be well placed at a competition. To help ensure success, some careful preparation work must be done before the event and the subsequent care of the horse during and after the competition will help ensure his well-being and therefore improve his performance. As previous chapters have already emphasized, horses require consistent care, but to simplify matters, we will look at the care of the horse before, during and after the day of competition.

The day before the competition

Tack and equipment This should be checked, assembled and cleaned. It is a good idea to compile a list of all the equipment that you are taking. You will find this particularly useful the next time you compete, as you will be able to identify what you need and what you don't need. For safety, it is advisable to check all stitching on your tack; particularly the

stitching of the girth straps, girth, stirrup leathers and the reins. For eventing, it is a good idea to take some spare equipment, especially a spare girth and a spare pair of reins.

The horse Your horse should be exercised as normal, unless he is travelling to the competition that day. As this is quite stressful, light exercise should be sufficient. You may wish to wash the horse, although this is best done a couple of days before the event to allow the coat to lie flat and give a better shine. Shoes should be checked daily, and it is better to have had the shoes on for at least a week, particularly if you are eventing, so that you know they are secure. All stud holes should be tapped (the threads are cleaned out) and either plugged with cotton wool or a road stud fitted. There is nothing worse than struggling to fit studs at a competition!

If the horse is eventing, some people like to cut down on the amount of hay fed a couple of days before, so that the horse

is not carrying too much bulk in his intestines, which could hinder him when galloping. There is no point in increasing the concentrate feed for extra energy the day before as it takes two or three days for food to be properly digested. Feed should be gradually increased during the training programme if more energy is required.

The trailer or lorry These should be checked and prepared as described in Chapter 12. It is amazing how many people forget to fill their car or lorry with fuel the day before, only to find that most petrol stations are closed when they leave for the competition at the crack of dawn! Your preparations the day before should be such that all you have to do in the morning is prepare the horse, load and go.

Equipment Check List

- First aid kits; both human and equine.
- All tack required. Check rule book to see what is allowed.
- Feed, hay, water and buckets. If staying away; bedding and mucking out tools.
- Grooming kit and plaiting equipment.
- Studs and stud tap. A nail to clean out stud holes and a small spanner.
- Documentation. Vaccination certificates or F.E.I. Passports may be required. It is also a good idea to take your confirmation of entry.
- Rider's clothes: check rule books to see what is required and allowed.

Competition Day

The best advice on competition days is: allow plenty of time. This will reflect in your performance all day; when you are relaxed, you can help calm your horse. It is very frustrating to find yourself sitting in an unexpected traffic jam, knowing that you are going to be late. The horse will be more settled if he has had a good and steady journey and being there a little early will enable you to find out where everything is located.

Working-in This can vary from horse to horse. It is very true to say that the horse that is calm and relaxed at competitions is the one to keep! Some horses will fizz up, whilst others will become nervous and slightly nappy. It is worth exerimenting with different working-in programmes until you find one that suits your horse. Some will require only 20–30 minutes before competing, whereas others will need to be brought out and worked two or three times.

Feeding Feed and water the horse during the day, sticking to his normal routine as closely as possible. However, if you are going cross country, then feed should be withheld two or three hours prior to starting due to the close proximity of the stomach to the diaphragm. Water should also be restricted, but if it is hot, it is essential that the horse gets fluid regularly. In any case, the rule of feeding at least one hour before work applies.

Washing down and grooming

This should be carried out if time allows between classes. If it is hot, washing the horse down is both refreshing and cooling. If jumping, keep a check on his legs for heat or cuts between classes. When you have finished classes that require the horse to be plaited, take the plaits out and dampen the mane thoroughly. This will help get rid of the curls.

Tack and equipment These should be cleaned and put away when finished with. There tends to be quite a lot of waiting around at competitions, so it is a good idea to sort out and clean as much equipment

as possible while you wait. This makes life a lot easier, particularly if you compete often.

Travelling home At the end of the day dress the horse to travel, give him a haynet and offer him a drink of water. If you have been competing in a cross country event, it is essential that you walk the horse until he has stopped blowing and possibly graze him in hand until he has cooled off. Many people will apply a cooling lotion to the horse's legs, to reduce swelling. When you arrive home, care for him as described in Chapter 12.

The day after

Check the horse for any cuts or bruises and trot the horse up to check that it is sound. If the horse normally goes out in the field, turn him out for a couple of hours. If he is not turned out, he must be lightly exercised so that he does not stiffen up. Pack away all your equipment and make sure that you leave the trailer or lorry mucked out, allowing the floor to dry.

APPENDIX II
FEEDING AND FITNESS PROGRAMME FOR A HORSE IN GENERAL WORK

Chapters 7 and 8 give an outline to feeding and exercise and Chapter 2 describes how to bring a horse up from grass. The following fitness programme brings all the information together to give an outline of a suitable feeding and fitness programme for a horse in general work, i.e. hacking, riding school work or schooling.

The horse

- 15hh Thoroughbred/Welsh cob
- 8 years old
- Calm temperament
- Weight: 400 kg

The horse has been living out in the field and doing light work; possibly hacking twice a week. He is now to be stabled and has been cared for as described in Chapter 2. The program is six weeks long. This will allow enough time to reduce his weight and build sufficient muscle to cope with general work. The type of work will condition all his connective tissues;

namely the skin, muscles, bones, ligaments and tendons.

Feeding

Total daily intake = 2.5 per cent of his body weight
2.5 per cent of 400 kg = **10 kg per day**

To work out the horse's weight you really require a weighbridge. However, it is possible to buy a special tape from your saddler or feed merchant that calculates the horse's weight by a measurement taken from the horse's girth.

Fig. 71 gives a table of feeds and their nutritional values. From this you can select the best type of mixtures of feeds. DE signifies the digestible energy value of the feed, so higher values give more energy. This horse is to be fed horse and pony cubes with chaff mixed in as he is not doing any work that requires a lot of energy. The protein level of this type of cube is about 10 per cent, which is more than adequate for a mature horse doing this type of work.

Week One

Feed Ad lib hay. This must be dampened to prevent coughing. Two small feeds can be given of ½ kg cubes mixed with chaff. The ad lib hay mimics the natural feeding of the horse and the small amount of concentrates allows the digestive system to get accustomed to the feed.

Exercise At the beginning of the week, the horse should be walk ridden for about twenty minutes. If you think that the horse may be excitable, then lunge him first. Otherwise work on circles should be avoided, as it is too stressful at this stage. By the end of the week the horse should be walking for about one hour. To begin with road work is the best type of exercise as the slight concussive effect of the hard surface will help to strengthen the bones, ligaments and tendons (see Chapter 8).

Week Two

Feeding The diet should be cut so that the horse is not receiving more than his total daily requirement; in this case 10 kg. This is particularly important if he is fat as you must reduce his weight for his health. The diet should still be high in fibre, with fibre to concentrates fed in a ratio of 80:20. This means about 8 kg per day in hay and bulk feed and 2 kg in concentrates. If the horse is still going out in the field, then this should be taken into account and his hay ration cut accordingly.

Exercise Exercise should be as week one, although you may wish to include slight gradients. It is very boring to walk for so long, but it will pay dividends as the horse gets fitter, as his body will be well-conditioned.

Week Three

Feeding This will be the same as week two, as you want the horse to lose some fat. If he is not carrying much weight, then you may increase the concentrate ration by 1 kg per day.

Exercise The horse should be doing at least one and a half hour's work daily. Roadwork should still be used, but you should expect the horse to work more actively, and definitely include hill work. You can trot for two or three minutes, but work on softer ground if possible.

Week Four

Feeding If you haven't already done so, increase the concentrate ration by 1 kg per day and cut the hay, so the horse is receiving 7 kg of hay per day and 3 kg of concentrate.

Exercise Work the horse as in week three, but increase the work time to two hours. You may include more trotting work; probably five to ten minutes, divided up into two-to-three minutes' bursts.

Week Five

Feeding Feed as in week four, unless the horse is losing a bit too much condition; in which case increase the concentrate ration by 1 kg per day. The feed that he is getting should provide more than adequate levels of energy and protein for the work he is doing. If the horse did come up from the field fat, it is particularly important not to overfeed in the early stages. The fitness programme is also a conditioning programme; a fat horse is an unhealthy horse.

Exercise As week four, but increase the total trot time to 20 minutes per day. Still trot in short bursts and preferably on softer going to reduce concussion, but include hills. This will help develop muscle and stamina.

Week Six

Feeding Increase the concentrate ration if necessary. The horse should be on a concentrate to fibre ratio of 60:40. Some will manage on less concentrates, some may need more.

Exercise The total work time is still two hours per day, although you may wish to spend half an hour of this schooling. Short bursts of canter can be included; about two-to-three minutes long. The horse is now fit enough to work as you wish. Its skin, bones, muscles, ligaments and tendons are conditioned to withstand work. Because the horse is stronger, its co-ordination is better, so it will cope with schooling on the flat and over fences. At this stage you may wish to extend the fitness programme to develop the horse's strength and stamina. This would involve using more canter work and hill work. This should not be necessary unless you wish to event or hunt.

Fig 71 Nutritional Values of Feed Stuffs

	DE	Crude Protein (%)	Ca (%)	P (%)
Oats	13	11	0.09	0.37
Barley	15	10	0.08	0.40
Maize	16	9	0.05	0.26
Sugar Beet Pulp	12	9	0.75	0.10
Wheat Bran	11	17	0.12	1.45
Horse and Pony Cube	10	10	Balanced	
Competition Cubes	13	13	Balanced	
Good seed hay	10	10	0.50	0.25
Meadow Hay	8	9	0.50	0.25

DE = Digestible Energy which is measured in Megajoules (MJ) per kilogram
Ca = Calcium
P = Phosphorus
Note: For healthy bone development, the calcium:phosporous ratio should be 2:1. This should be taken into account when combining feedstuffs. The compound feed manufacturer should balance this for you.

BIBLIOGRAPHY

Adams, O.R., *Lameness in Horses* (Lea & Febiger, USA, 1974)

British Horse Society, *Manual of Stable Management* (1950, reprinted 1990)

Bromily, Mary, *Equine Injury and Therapy* (Blackwell Scientific, 1987)

Cunha, Tony, *Horse Feeding and Nutrition* (Academic Press, 2nd edition 1991)

Dennis, E., *Colour Atlas of Equine Parasites* (Baillière Tindall, 1986)

Frape, D., *Equine Nutrition & Feeding* (Longman, 1986)

Hartley Edwards, E., *Saddlery* (J.A. Allen, 1987)

Hayes, Captain M. Horace, *Veterinary Notes for Horse Owners* (Stanley Paul, 1987, revised by Peter Rossdale FRCVS)

Hickman, J., & Humphrey, M., *Hickman's Farriery* (J.A. Allen, 2nd edition 1988)

Houghton-Brown, J., & Powell-Smith, V., *Horse & Stable Management* (Blackwell Scientific, 1984)

Launder, D., & Lucas, D., *Feeding Facts* (D.J. Murphy, 1986)

McCarthy, Gillian, *Pasture Management for Horses and Ponies* (Blackwell Scientific, 1987)

Mortimer, Monty, *The Horse Owner's Handbook* (David & Charles, 1987)

Pavord, Tony & Fisher, Rod *The Equine Veterinary Manual* (Crowood Press, 1987)

Pilliner, S., *Getting your Horse Fit* (Blackwell Scientific, 1986)

Rees, Lucy, *The Horse's Mind* (Stanley Paul, 1984)

Rossdale, Peter, *The Horse from Conception to Maturity* (J.A. Allen, 1984)

Rossdale, Peter, & Wreford, Susan, *The Horse's Health from A – Z* (David & Charles, 1989)

Smythe R.H., *The Horse, Structure and Movement* (J.A. Allen, 1967, second edition revised by Goody, P.C., 1972)

Tuke, Diana, *Bit by Bit* (J.A. Allen, 1973)

Tuke, Diana, *Stitch by Stitch* (J.A. Allen, 1977)

Vogel, C., *How to keep your horse healthy* (Blackwell Scientific, 1989)

Wyn Jones, G., *Equine Lameness* (Blackwell Scientific, 1988)

EQUESTRIAN SUPPLIERS AND FURTHER STUDY

The horse industry is continuing to expand rapidly. There are many openings in the industry at different levels and in different spheres. The industry requires people with a range of skills; be it as a yard manager or publicity officer. There are various institutions and societies in the United Kingdom that offer examinations and courses for those wishing to pursue a career with horses.

Societies

Association of British Riding Schools, Old Brewery Yard, Penzance, Cornwall TR18 2SL

British Horse Society, British Equestrian Centre, Stoneleigh, Warwickshire, CV8 2LR

National Pony Society, Brook House, 25 High Street, Alton, Hampshire GU34 1AW

Colleges

Bicton College of Agriculture, East Budleigh, Budleigh Salterton EX9 7BY.

Bishop Burton College of Agriculture, Bishop Burton, Beverley, North Humberside HU17 8QG

Brackenhurst College, Brackenhurst, Southwell, Nottinghamshire NG25 0GF

Cambridge College of Agriculture, Landbeach Road, Milton, Cambridge CB4 6DB

Cannington College, Cannington, Bridgewater, Somerset TA5 2LS

Clinterty Agricultural College, Kinellar AB5 0TN

Cordwainers College, 182 Mare Street, London E8 3RE

Duchy College, Stoke Climsland, Callington, Cornwall PL17 8PB

Lancashire College of Agriculture, Myerscough Hall, Bilsborrow, Preston, Lancs PR3 0RY

Lincolnshire College of Agriculture, Caythorpe Court, Grantham, Lincs NG32 3EP

Moulton College, Moulton, Northampton NN3 1RR

Oatridge Agricultural College, Ecclesmachan, Broxburn, West Lothian EH52 6NH

Plumpton Agricultural College, Plumpton, Lewes, East Sussex BN7 3AE

The Royal Veterinary College, University of London, Royal College Street, Camden Town, London NW1 0TU

Warwickshire College of Agriculture, Moreton Hall, Moreton Morrell, Warwickshire CV35 9BL

West Oxfordshire College, Holloway Road, Witney, Oxfordshire OX8 7EE

West Sussex College of Agriculture, Brinsbury, North Heath, Pulborough, Sussex RH20 1DL

Worcestershire College of Agriculture, Hindlip, Worcester WR3 8SS

Writtle Agricultural College, Chelmsford, Essex CM1 3RR

Training Centres

Brampton Stables, Church Brampton, Northampton

Catherston Stud, Black Knoll House, Brockenhurst, Hampshire S042 7QE

Huntley School of Equitation, Wood End Farm, Gloucestershire GL19 3EY

Loughton Manor Equestrian Centre, Redland Drive, Childs Way, Loughton, Milton Keynes, Buckinghamshire MK5 8AZ

Leigh Equestrian Centre, Three Gates, Leigh, Sherborne, Dorset

Snainton Riding Centre, Snainton, near Scarborough, North Yorkshire

The Talland School of Equitation, Church Farm, Siddington, Cirencester, Gloucestershire

Wellington Riding Limited, Basingstoke Road, Heckfield, Basingstoke, Hampshire

Yorkshire Riding Centre, Markington, Harrogate, North Yorkshire HG3 3PE

Open Learning

Briar Enterprises, The Old Barn, Felsham Rd, Cockfield, Bury St Edmunds, Suffolk, IP30 0LP

Equi-study, The David & Charles Equestrian College, Brunel House, Freepost, Newton Abbot, Devon

Equestrian suppliers and services

Ardern Sales Ltd, 28C London Road, Alderley Edge, Cheshire SK9 7DZ. Horse-box suppliers

A.D.A.S, Block 2, Government Buildings, Lawnswood, Leeds LS16 5PY. Equine Consultancy Service, specialists in land management

Badminton Horse Feeds, 3A West Market Place, Cirencester, Gloucestershire. Manufacturers of horse feeds

Baileys Horse Feeds, Four Elms Mill, Bardfield Sailing, Braintree, Essex

British Equestrian Insurance Ltd, Hildenbrook House, The Slade, Tonbridge, Kent TH9 1HY. Equestrian insurance specialists

Cottage Craft, Cottage Industries Ltd, Crown Lane, Wychbold, Droitwich, Worcestershire WR9 0BX. Manufacturers of equestrian equipment

Diceabed International Ltd, Haven House, Haven Bank, Haven Road, Exeter, EX2 8BP. Manufacturers of paper bedding

The General Chip Co., Denver Site, Ferry Lane, Rainham, Essex RM13 9BU. Manufacturers of wood shavings for bedding

Dodson & Horrell Ltd, Ringstead, Kettering, Northants NN14 4BX. Feed merchants and consultants

Equine Research Station, Balaton Lodge, Newmarket, Suffolk

Equivite, 180 Aztec West, Almondsbury, Bristol Avon BS12 4TH. Manufacturers of feed supplements

Horse Requisites Newmarket Ltd, Black Bear Lane, Newmarket, Suffolk CB8 0JT. Mail-order suppliers of equestrian equipment

HorseHage, Mark Westaway & Son, Love Lane Farm, Marldon, Paignton, Devon, Manufacturers of pre-packed hay

Loddon Livestock Ltd, Beccles Rd, Loddon, Norfolk NR14 6JJ. Manufacturers of stabling, and fencing specialists

Old Basing Saddlery, 69 The Street, Old Basing, Basingstoke, Hampshire RG24 0BY. Saddlery and riding-wear shop, with mail-order service

Rice Trailer Centre, Allens Caravans, Wootton Hall, Wootton Wawen, Henley-in-Arden, Warwickshire B95 6EE. Manufacturers of horse trailers

Sinclair Trailers Ltd, Wargate Bridge, Gosberton, Spalding, Lincolnshire PE11 4HH. Manufacturers of horse trailers

Spillers Horse & Speciality Feeds, 180 Aztec West, Almondsbury, Bristol, Avon. Manufacturers of horse feeds; consultants

Swaine & Adeney, 185 Piccadilly, London W1V 0HA. Saddlery suppliers with mail-order service

Wyvern Equestrian Specialist Books, Wyvern House, 6 The Business Park, Ely, Cambridgeshire CB6 4JW. Equestrian Book Club

GLOSSARY

ABSCESS – a localized collection of pus caused by infection.

ACUTE – the severe stage of a disease.

ALBUMIN – serum protein present in the blood plasma.

ANAEMIA – a deficiency of haemoglobin, the iron-containing protein in red blood cells.

ANTERIOR MESENTERIC ARTERY – supplies small intestines, part of the colon and the caecum.

AORTA – the trunk of main artery.

ARTERY – a blood vessel that carries oxygenated blood from the heart to the rest of the horse's body.

ASCARID – a nematode parasite to be found in small intestine.

ATRIUM – one of upper chambers of heart which receive blood from the veins and pass it to the lower, pumping chambers (**ventricles**).

AZOTURIA – a condition affecting the large muscle mass of the back and hind quarters.

BARS: (1) – in the foot: continuation of the wall **(2)** in the mouth: sensitive areas on which the bit lies.

BASOPHIL – white blood cells.

BICUSPID VALVE – the valve separating the left atrium and the left ventricle in the heart.

BLISTERING – to induce severe inflammation to the skin to speed healing.

BLOOD – the fluid that circulates through the circulatory system. Takes nutrients to the tissue and waste to the kidneys.

BLOOD TEST – a laboratory test to diagnose disease and monitor performance.

BOX-WALKING – relentless walking around the box, regarded as a vice.

BRUSHING – striking the fetlock region of the opposite leg.

BRONCHUS – the air passage into the lungs.

BURSA – a sac or cavity which secretes a lubricating fluid, thus reducing friction around joints or where tendons pass over bones.

BURSAL ENGLARGEMENT – a soft visible swelling; often around joints.

CAECUM – collecting chamber for the large intestine.

CALCIUM – mineral required for bone and tooth formation.

CALKIN – a square of metal found on the outside heel of a shoe to aid grip.

CARBOHYDRATE – a food substance found in animal and vegetable tissue which forms an important part of the diet, contributing mainly energy.

CARBON DIOXIDE – a gaseous waste product of aerobic respiration.

CARDIAC MUSCLE – muscle of the heart.

CELLULOSE – found in plant stems; the 'roughage' in many foodstuffs. It breaks down to form carbohydrates.

CHRONIC – a disease of long duration.

CORIUM – modified vascular tissue at the top of the hoof.

CORONET BAND – found at the top of the hoof. Seat of hoof growth.

CRIB-BITING – where horse grabs a fixed object with his front teeth. Can be controlled by a 'crib strap'.

CRUPPER – piece of tack fitted to prevent saddle slipping forward.

DIGESTIBLE ENERGY – energy value of food. Measured in megajoules.

DIGITAL CUSHION – the fibro-elastic pad found underneath the pedal bone.

ELECTROLYTE – minerals that have ionized in fluid. Play an important role in body processes.

ENDOTOXIN – poison produced in the body.

ENTIRE – another name for a stallion.

ENZYME – a protein which acts as a catalyst.

EOSINOPHIL – type of white blood cell.

EPIGLOTTIS – small flap of cartilage that covers the entrance to the larynx to prevent food from entering during swallowing.

EPIPHYSIS – growing sector found at the end of bones. Separated in young horses by cartilage.

EPISTAXIS – nosebleed.

ERYTHROCYTE – red blood cell.

EXCRETION – the removal of waste products from the horse's body.

EXOSTOSIS – an abnormal deposit of bone, usually as response to inflammation or trauma.

FAT – material laid down around organs and muscles of the body. Also forms part of diet.

FIBRE – insoluble carbohydrate that forms an essential part of the diet.

FIBRIN – the essential fibrous protein portion of the blood.

FIBRINOGEN – a blood protein; essential for clotting.

FIRING – treatment used to produce a severe inflammation. Not often used today.

FLOATING – the act of filing teeth.

FROG – The 'V' shaped horny substance in the middle of the sole of the foot.

GALLS – sores caused by rubbing/friction.

GASTRIC – pertaining to the stomach.

GLANDS – aggregation of cells, specialized to produce hormones, digestive enzymes and sweat.

GLOBULINS – group of blood proteins.

GLUCOSE – a simple sugar essential for life.

GLYCOGEN – formed by carbohydrate. Primary energy store of the horse's body.

GLYCOLYSIS – the breakdown of glycogen to form energy.

HAEMATOMA – a localized collection of blood, usually due to damaged blood vessels.

HAEMOGLOBIN – the oxygen-carrying protein of blood.

HAEMORRHAGE – large escape of blood either internal or external.

HACKAMORE – a bitless bridle.

HAVERSIAN SYSTEM – the system that structures bone cells.

HEART – muscular organ with four chambers that pumps blood around the circulatory system.

HEAVES – a term used to describe the disease that results in the alveoli in the lungs being damaged, causing forced exhalation.

HISTAMINE – a hormone which dilates capillaries and constricts the smooth muscle of the lung.

HORMONE – a chemical produced in the body which effects the activity of a specific body organ.

HORSE-SICK – pastures which have been grazed for too long and are suspected of having a heavy infestation of parasites.

HYPERTROPHY – the enlargement or overgrowth of an organ, for example, the increase in muscle bulk due to sustained hard exercise.

ILEUM – part of the small intestine.

IMPACTION – the condition of being firmly lodged or wedged.

INFLAMMATION – a condition where tissues react to injury.

INFLUENZA – an acute viral disease of the respiratory tract.

INHALATION – to draw air into the lungs.

INTERVAL TRAINING – the training method that involves intervals of controlled stress on the body.

INTRACELLULAR FLUID – fluid found inside cells.

JEJUNUM – the middle portion of the small intestine.

LACTIC ACID – an organic acid produced by anaerobic muscle metabolism.

LAMENESS – the unevenness of stride.

LAMINAE – membrane containing fine leaf-like projections.

LARYNX – the voice box.

LETTING DOWN – reducing a horse's fitness.

LEUCOCYTES – white blood cells.

LIGAMENT – band of fibrous tissue that connects bones or cartilages.

LIGNIN – an indigestible structural carbohydrate found in plant cell walls.

LONG REINS – lunge lines or similar, usually 6–9m (20–30ft) long and suitable for long-reining.

LUNGWORM – parasite that lives in the air passages of the lungs.

LYMPH – a transparent yellowish liquid containing white blood cells.

LYMPHANGITIS – a disease that effects the lymphatic system.

LYMPHATIC SYSTEM – a system of vessels that carry lymph.

LYMPHOCYTE – a type of white blood cell.

LYSINE – an essential amino acid.

MARROW – red or yellow material found in central cavities of long bones.

MEGAJOULE – unit that measures the energy value of foodstuff.

MEMBRANE – a thin layer of tissue that lines, covers or divides a space in the body.

METABOLISM – the total physical and chemical activities of an animal.

METHIONINE – an essential amino acid.

MITOCHONDRIA – the powerhouse of the cell where energy is produced. They also contain genes.

MONOCYTES – white blood cells.

MONOSACCARIDE – a simple sugar.

MYOGLOBIN – protein that acts as a temporary store for oxygen in the muscles.

NAVICULAR BONE – a name given to the sesamoid bone in the foot.

NEUTROPHIL – a white blood cell.

OSMOSIS – diffusion through semipermeable membrane.

OSTEITIS – inflammation of the bone.

OSTEOBLASTS – cells involved with bone formation.

OSTEOCLASTS – cells involved with bone destruction.

OVER-REACH – a wound which occurs when the hind foot strikes the heel or back of the foreleg between the knee and heel.

PACKED CELL VOLUME – proportion of blood cells to plasma.

PEDAL BONE – also called coffin bone. Found in the hoof.

PERIOPLE – external varnish covering of the hoof.

PHARYNX – the space between the mouth and the oesophagus.

PLASMA – the liquid portion of blood.

POINTING – the term used to describe when a horse pushes a foreleg forward when resting to relieve pressure.

PROTEIN – a group of complex compounds containing nitrogen. Formed from amino acids.

PULMONARY – pertaining to the lungs.

QUARTERING – the term used to describe the light grooming of a horse in the morning.

QUIDDING – when the horse spits out half chewed food.

REMODELLING – the term used to describe the changes in bone.

RENAL ARTERY – supplies the kidneys with blood.

RING BONE – bony enlargement on the pastern bones.

ROUGHING OFF – procedure of turning a stabled horse away to grass.

SECRETE – to produce and give off cell products.

SERUM – clear fluid found in blood.

SESAMOID BONES – small bones over which tendons run.

SKELETAL MUSCLE – the striated voluntary muscle of the skeleton.

SMOOTH MUSCLE – involuntary muscle found in the digestive system.

SOFT PALATE – divides the pharynx and cuts off the cavity of the nose when swallowing.

SPEEDY CUTTING – a wound caused by the hoof of the opposite leg cutting in to the inside of the leg below the knee.

STARCH – the form in which plants store glucose.

STARING COAT – when the horse's coat stands on end. Usually signifies ill-health.

STALE – to urinate.

STRONGYLE – redworm.

STRAPPING – the thorough grooming of the stabled horse.

SYNOVIAL FLUID – lubricating fluid; found in joints.

SYSTEMIC CIRCULATION – the circulation of blood through the body.

TENDON – a fibrous chord made of the protein collagen that connects muscles to bones.

TENOBLASTS – cells involved in tendon destruction.

TENOCYTES – cells involved in tendon formation.

THATCHING – drying off a horse which has returned from work still hot by placing straw under a jute rug or sweat sheet.

TRACHEA – the windpipe.

UREA – a waste product discharged in urine.

VACCINE – a suspension of treated micro-organisms. Used to prevent disease.

VEIN – a vessel through which blood passes back to the heart.

VENTRICLES – two powerful lower chambers of the heart.

VILLI – tiny finger-like projections of a membrane.

WEAVING – the term used to describe a nervous disorder. The horse will swing from one foreleg to another.

WHISTLING – the term used to describe a horse making a noise during exhalation.

INDEX